Pr...ted ...
Ministry Of Islamic A...
and ...
With The Co-Opera...
Aziz Al-Braim V...

Rulings
Pertaining To
Muslim Women

By

Dr. Saleh Bin Fauzan Al-Fauzan

In English

Translated By

Burhan Loqueman

Printed Under the Supervision of:

The Deputyship For Printing And Publishing Affairs

1422 AH

© Ministry of Islamic Affairs, 2001

```
King Fahd National Library Cataloging-in-Publication Data
Al-Fozan, Salih Fozan
    Advisory notes on rulings pertaining believing .-Riyadh.
    152 p., 12x17 cm
    ISBN: 9960-29-347-5
    1- Faith (Islamic creeds)              I- Title
243 dc                                     4254/21
```

Legal Deposit No. 4254/21
ISBN : 9960-29-347-5

الطبعة الثانية
١٤٢٢هـ

بِسْمِ ٱللَّهِ ٱلرَّحْمَٰنِ ٱلرَّحِيمِ

Tables of Contents

Laws Which Protect The Nobility & Chastity Of A Woman

بِسْمِ ٱللَّهِ ٱلرَّحْمَٰنِ ٱلرَّحِيمِ

Introduction

All praise be to Allaah who decreed and guided, and created the pairs, male and female, from a single drop. I bear witness that there is no god worthy of worship except Allaah, alone without partners in worship. All praise be to Him firstly and lastly. I bear witness that Muhammad is his servant and messenger; he was raised to the heavens and shown the great Signs of his Lord. May the peace and blessings of Allaah be upon him, his family and companions, the virtuous, and the people of intellect.

The woman has been given a particular status in Islaam. Great importance is attached to her position, and the Prophet, may the peace and blessings of Allaah be upon him used to give special guidance to women, and left his guidance for them in his speech at 'Arafaat. These points prove that it is compulsory to pay special attention to women at all times, and in particular today, when the Muslim woman has been singled out for attack, in order to deprive her of her nobility and status. It is therefore incumbent to warn women of these dangers and explain to them the path of success.

I hope this book will be a pointer to this path, as it contains some of the Islaamic laws specific to woman. The book is a small contribution; a small effort, and I hope that Allaah makes it beneficial despite its smallness. The book is the first step on this path after which, it is hoped, greater and more expansive steps are taken to achieve what is better.

I have divided this work into the following sections:

Chapter 1

General Laws

1. The status of a woman before the age of Islaam

The period before Islaam is known as the *Jaahiliyyah* period (literally, the 'Period of Ignorance'), which refers to the culture of all the nations of the world generally, and in particular the culture of the Arabs. This was the period when mankind was in a state of an intermission of Prophethood, and the disappearance of the ways of guidance. As has been related in hadeeth, Allaah looked at the people, and abhorred them, both the Arabs and the non-Arabs among them, except for a few remnants of the People of the Book (the Jews and the Christians).

Women at this time generally lived oppressed lives, particularly in Arab society; the birth of a girl for example was an unwelcome event - to the point where they used to bury their daughters alive. Others left them to live oppressed and miserable lives. This was as Allaah said:

﴾ وَإِذَا بُشِّرَ أَحَدُهُم بِٱلْأُنثَىٰ ظَلَّ وَجْهُهُ مُسْوَدًّا وَهُوَ كَظِيمٌ ۝ يَتَوَٰرَىٰ مِنَ ٱلْقَوْمِ مِن سُوٓءِ مَا بُشِّرَ بِهِۦٓ أَيُمْسِكُهُۥ عَلَىٰ هُونٍ أَمْ يَدُسُّهُۥ فِى ٱلتُّرَابِ أَلَا سَآءَ مَا يَحْكُمُونَ ۝ ﴿

"And when news is brought to one of them of (the birth) of a female (child), his face becomes dark, and he is filled with inward grief. He hides himself from his people with shame, because of the bad news he has had! Shall he keep her with dishonour and contempt or bury her in the dust? Certainly evil is their decision." [Al-Nahl: 58-59].

And Allaah the Most High said:

﴾ وَإِذَا ٱلْمَوْءُۥدَةُ سُئِلَتْ ۝ بِأَىِّ ذَنۢبٍ قُتِلَتْ ۝ ﴿

"And when the female (infant) buried alive is questioned; for what crime she was killed". [Al-Takwir: 8-9]

If the girl was spared the fate of being buried alive and was allowed to live, she lived an oppressed life. Only males used to inherit, and the woman did not receive a share of the inheritance of her relatives, no matter how rich they were, or how poor and needy she might herself be. In fact, she herself was regarded as her husband's property and was inherited along with the rest of his wealth upon his death!

The number of wives a man was allowed to have was not limited, so at times many women lived under one husband - without regard for the effect this would have on the women or the oppression, problems and pressures placed on the wives.

2. The status of women during the age of Islaam

When Islaam appeared, it removed this oppression of women and returned to them their proper status in Mankind. Allaah says:

$$ \text{﴿ يَٰٓأَيُّهَا ٱلنَّاسُ إِنَّا خَلَقْنَٰكُم مِّن ذَكَرٍ وَأُنثَىٰ ﴾} $$

'O people! Indeed we created you from a male and a female.' [Al-Hujurat: 13]

So Allaah has stated that the woman is an equal partner of the man in terms of reward and punishment for their actions. Allaah says:

$$ \text{﴿ مَنْ عَمِلَ صَٰلِحًا مِّن ذَكَرٍ أَوْ أُنثَىٰ وَهُوَ مُؤْمِنٌ فَلَنُحْيِيَنَّهُۥ حَيَوٰةً طَيِّبَةً وَلَنَجْزِيَنَّهُمْ أَجْرَهُم بِأَحْسَنِ مَا كَانُوا۟ يَعْمَلُونَ ﴾} $$

"Whoever works righteousness, whether male or female, while he (or she) is true believer, verily to him We will give a good and pure life (in this world), and

We will bestow on such their reward according to the best of their actions." [Al-Nahl: 97]

And He, the Most High says:

$$﴿ لِيُعَذِّبَ ٱللَّهُ ٱلْمُنَٰفِقِينَ وَٱلْمُنَٰفِقَٰتِ وَٱلْمُشْرِكِينَ وَٱلْمُشْرِكَٰتِ ﴾$$

"So that Allaah will punish the hypocrites, men and women, and the unbelievers, men and women." [Al-Ahzab: 73]

Allaah decreed it haraam (illegal) that a woman be treated as part of her deceased husband's inheritance. He said:

$$﴿ يَٰٓأَيُّهَا ٱلَّذِينَ ءَامَنُوا۟ لَا يَحِلُّ لَكُمْ أَن تَرِثُوا۟ ٱلنِّسَآءَ كَرْهًا ﴾$$

"O you who believe! You are forbidden to inherit women against their will." [An-Nisa: 19]

So He guaranteed for the woman her independence and made her an inheritor - not something to be inherited, and declared her right: a set portion from the inheritance of her husband and her near relations: He said:

12

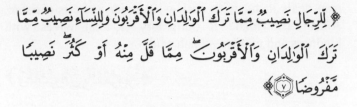

﴿ لِّلرِّجَالِ نَصِيبٌ مِّمَّا تَرَكَ ٱلۡوَٰلِدَانِ وَٱلۡأَقۡرَبُونَ وَلِلنِّسَآءِ نَصِيبٌ مِّمَّا تَرَكَ ٱلۡوَٰلِدَانِ وَٱلۡأَقۡرَبُونَ مِمَّا قَلَّ مِنۡهُ أَوۡ كَثُرَ نَصِيبًا مَّفۡرُوضًا ۞ ﴾

"There is share for men and a share for women from what is left by parents and those nearest related, whether the property be small large, - a determinate share." [An-Nisa: 7]

And He also said:

﴿ يُوصِيكُمُ ٱللَّهُ فِيٓ أَوۡلَٰدِكُمۡ لِلذَّكَرِ مِثۡلُ حَظِّ ٱلۡأُنثَيَيۡنِ فَإِن كُنَّ نِسَآءً فَوۡقَ ٱثۡنَتَيۡنِ فَلَهُنَّ ثُلُثَا مَا تَرَكَ وَإِن كَانَتۡ وَٰحِدَةً فَلَهَا ٱلنِّصۡفُ ﴾

"Allah commands you as regards your (children's) inheritance: to the male a portion equal to that of two females; if (there are) only daughters, two or more, their share is two-thirds of the inheritance; if only one, her share is a half." [An-Nisa: 11]

- to the end of what was revealed regarding the inheritance of a woman, in her position as a mother, a daughter, a sister, or a wife.

In the area of polygamy, Allaah decreed an upper limit of four wives, and that on the condition that the man deals justly with each wife as far as he is capable. Allaah also made it obligatory to treat wives with kindness and equity: Allaah said:

﴿ وَعَاشِرُوهُنَّ بِٱلْمَعْرُوفِ ﴾

"And live with them on a footing of kindness and equity." [An-Nisa: 19]

And He decreed the bridal money as a right of the woman, and ordered that it be paid to her in full, except what she may decide to grant out of a generous heart and her own good pleasure: He said:

﴿ وَءَاتُواْ ٱلنِّسَآءَ صَدُقَٰتِهِنَّ نِحْلَةً فَإِن طِبْنَ لَكُمْ عَن شَىْءٍ مِّنْهُ نَفْسًا فَكُلُوهُ هَنِيٓئًا مَّرِيٓئًا ﴾

"And give the women (on marriage) their bridal money as a free gift; but if they of their own good pleasure remit any part of it to you, take it and enjoy it without fear of any harm." [An-Nisa: 4]

Allaah made the woman a guardian, one who orders, one who prohibits, within the house of her husband, and an authority over her children. The Prophet, may the peace and blessings of Allaah be upon him said: 'The woman is guardian (or custodian) in the house of her husband and she is responsible for her flock.'

And He made it obligatory on the husband to provide for her and cloth her with equity and honour.

14

3. The desires of the enemies of Islaam and their lackeys with regard to stripping the Muslim woman of her honour and rights

Today, the enemies of Islaam, in fact the enemies of Mankind, from among the disbelievers, the hypocrites and those who have in their hearts a sickness are infuriated with the nobility, status and protection which the Muslim woman has been granted in Islaam. This is because the enemies of Islaam and the hypocrites seek to make the woman an instrument of destruction; a snare by which they can entrap those who are weak in their imaan (faith) and those who have bodily desires in order that they satisfy their desperate lusts. As Allaah says:

﴿ وَيُرِيدُ ٱلَّذِينَ يَتَّبِعُونَ ٱلشَّهَوَٰتِ أَن تَمِيلُواْ مَيْلًا عَظِيمًا ﴾

"But the wish of those who follow their lusts is that you should deviate away (from the Right path), - far, far away." [An-Nisa: 27]

Those among the Muslims who have a sickness in their hearts wish to transform the woman into a cheap commodity in the marketplace of the desirous and satanic temptations. They wish to make her a commodity displayed in front of their eyes so that they can enjoy her beauty and exact from her what is far worse.

For this reason, they have tried hard to remove the woman from her home to join the men in the workplace, side by side, or to serve men as nurses in hospitals, as hostesses on planes, as teachers or students in mixed classrooms, as actresses in theatres, singers, as presenters in various forms of media, spreading fitna (corruption) with her voice and her appearance.

Licentious magazines use pictures of naked young women as a means to spread and sell their publications. Traders and manufacturers have also used these images as a means to sell their goods, by displaying them in their advertisements and on their goods.

Because of these dangerous developments, the woman has been removed from her original role in the house. As a result, the husband is obligated to find a maid to bring up his children and to run the affairs of the house. This has in turn caused much fitna, and produced many more evils.

However, we do not prohibit the woman from working outside her house provided the following conditions are met:

♦ **She must really need to work,** or the society has a definite need for her to work, if there are no others who can undertake her type of work.

♦ **That this work takes second place to her duties in the house,** which is her original and primary role.

♦ **That her work be involved with women only**, such as teaching women, or being a doctor or nurse for women, and that she be separated from men.

Also, there is no harm for the woman to learn what she is required to know of her religion; it is in fact obligatory upon her to do so. There is nothing wrong if she is taught with other women, and she may attend lessons in the Masjid, and other similar places, as long as she is properly veiled and separated from men, according to the pattern set by the women of the pioneer Islamic society in the way they used to work, study, and attend the Masjid.

Chapter 2

Laws Pertaining To The Beautification Of The Body

The woman must perform the required actions relating to her fitra (original state of purity) which is specific and appropriate to her as a woman.

This includes cutting her nails and taking care of them. This is because trimming the nails is a Sunnah by the consensus of the scholars of Islaam, as it is part of the fitra that has been specified in the hadeeth of the Prophet, may the peace and blessings of Allaah be upon him. Other reasons include the hygienic advantages resulting from the removal of excess nail, coupled with the fact that leaving the nails to grow long is ugly and resembles the claws of beasts of prey. Dirt collects underneath the nails, and long nails prevent water, used for ablution, from reaching what is underneath them.

Some Muslim women, because of their blind following of the disbelieving women and their ignorance of the Sunnah, have adopted the practice of growing their nails long.

It is also Sunnah for the woman to remove the hair from her armpits and pubic regions, in accordance with the hadeeth narrated regarding this practice, and in accordance with personal hygiene and good appearance.

It is better to perform this every week, and it should not be left longer than forty days.

The prohibitions regarding her hair and eyebrows, and the ruling regarding dyeing and tinting the hair.

i) The woman is required to grow her hair long, and it is not permissible for her to shave her head, except in cases of extreme necessity. Shaykh Muhammad ibn Ibraheem Aal Shaykh, the Mufti of Saudi Arabia, may Allaah have mercy on him, said:

> And as for the hair of the heads of the women, it is not permissible for it to be shaved, because of the hadeeth related by Nasaa'i in his Sunan with his isnaad (chain of narration) from 'Ali, may Allah be pleased with him; and al-Bazaar also narrated it with his isnaad in his Musnad from 'Uthmaan; Ibn Jareer also narrated it with his isnaad from 'Ikrimah, they said: 'The Messenger of Allaah, may the peace and blessings of Allaah be upon him prohibited the woman from shaving her head. A prohibition from the Prophet, may the peace and blessings of Allaah be upon him indicates that the act prohibited is haraam, provided there is no other proof to indicate otherwise.'

Mulla 'Ali, may Allah be pleased with him Qaari stated in *al-Mirqah sharh al-Mishkaat:*

... (concerning) the Prophet, may the peace and blessings of Allaah be upon him's statement, '...that the woman shaves her head...', this is because the braids of a woman are like the beard of a man in terms of beauty and appearance.[1]

As for shortening the hair, if there is a need for this to be done other than beautification, for example, she is unable to look after it or it becomes very long and difficult for her to manage, then there is no harm for her to trim her hair within the limits of her need. Some of the wives of the Prophet, may the peace and blessings of Allaah be upon him did so after the Prophet's death, may the peace and blessings of Allaah be upon him, as they had no need to beautify themselves, and thus they did not need to grow their hair long.

However, if the intention in cutting her hair is to imitate the disbelieving or sinful women, or to imitate men, then cutting her hair in this case is haraam without any doubt, because of the prohibition of imitating the disbelievers in general, and the prohibition of women to imitate men.

If the intention is to beautify herself, then there is every reason to say that it is not permissible. Our Shaykh, Muhammad Ameen ash-Shanqeeti, may Allaah have mercy upon him said:

---

1 *Majmu' al-Fataawa ash-Shaykh Muhammad ibn Ibraheem* [2/49].

The custom that has become prevalent in many countries, of a woman cutting her hair close to the roots of her hair, is a western practice -contradictory to the practice of Muslim women and the women of the Arabs before Islaam. Thus, it is among the deviations whose evils have spread among people, in their religion, their behaviour, style and other areas.

Then he explained the hadeeth that, '...the wives of the Prophet, may the peace and blessings of Allaah be upon him used to cut hair from their heads until they looked like wafra...'[2]:

The wives of the Prophet, may the peace and blessings of Allaah be upon him cut their hair after the death of the Prophet, may the peace and blessings of Allaah be upon him because they used to beautify themselves for him during his lifetime -and from their most gorgeous symbols of beauty was their hair. But after his death his wives were given a special ruling – unique to them among all the women of the earth -and that was: they were not permitted to marry ever again, they were to abandon the hope of ever marrying again. So they were like the women who are in their 'Iddah (period of mourning) after the death of the Prophet, may the peace and blessings of Allaah be upon him, up to the time of their death. Allaah says:

---

2 *Wafra*: The Arabic name given to the shape of the hair when it is left to reach the top lobe of the ear.

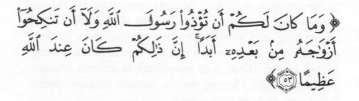

﴿ وَمَا كَانَ لَكُمْ أَن تُؤْذُواْ رَسُولَ ٱللَّهِ وَلَا أَن تَنكِحُوٓاْ أَزْوَجَهُ مِنۢ بَعْدِهِۦ أَبَدًا إِنَّ ذَٰلِكُمْ كَانَ عِندَ ٱللَّهِ عَظِيمًا ﴿٥٣﴾ ﴾

"And it is not (right) for you that you should annoy Allah's Messenger, nor that you should ever marry his wives after him (his death). Verily, with Allah that shall be an enormity." [Al-Ahzab: 53]

And abandoning the hope of marrying men totally is the reason why an exception was made for leaving some acts associated with beautification, which would not have been allowed for other than that reason.

So it is obligatory on a woman to safeguard her hair and take care of it. She could make it into plaits, but it is not permissible for her to gather it above her head or make it into a bun at the nape of her neck. Shaykh Al-Islaam, Ibn Taymiyyah stated in *Majmu' al-Fataawa* [22/145]:

…As some of the loose women do, they make their hair into a single plait, which hangs down between their shoulders.

Shaykh Muhammad ibn Ibraheem, Mufti of Saudi Arabia said:

…Regarding what some of the Muslim women do at this time, like tying the hair to one side and gathering it to the back of her head, or tying it above her head, as western women do, this is not permissible as it involves imitating the women of the disbelievers.

It is narrated from Abu Hurairah, may Allah be pleased with him in a long hadeeth that he said: 'The Messenger of Allaah, may the peace and blessings of Allaah be upon him said: 'There are two types of the People of the Fire I did not see; men with whips like the tails of cows, beating people with them, and women that are 'clothed' but naked, flirtatious women[3], their heads are like the humps of lean camels – they will never enter paradise, and they will never smell its fragrance, even though its fragrance can be smelt from such-and-such a distance.'" Narrated by Muslim. Some of the scholars have explained his statement, '...their heads are like the humps of lean camels', meaning that they style their hair to one side, and this is the style of loose women. Other women also style their hair in this way, which is a style of western women, and those Muslim women who imitate them.

In the same way that the Muslim woman is not allowed to shave her hair or cut it unnecessarily, she is also not allowed to join her hair with false hair (i.e. wear a wig). This is because of what has been narrated in Bukhaari and Muslim, 'The Messenger of Allaah, may the peace and blessings of Allaah be upon him cursed the woman who joins her hair with false hair, and the one that does that for another woman;' this is because of the dishonesty involved in this action. An example of this is to wear a wig, which is prevalent today. Bukhaari and Muslim and others have narrated that Mu'aawiyah,

---

3 Meaning that they are astray and deviated and cause others to deviate.

may Allaah be please with him, gave a speech when he came to Madeena and he took out a lock of hair and said: 'What is wrong with your women, placing something like this in their hair? I heard the Messenger of Allaah, may the peace and blessings of Allaah be upon him say, "Any woman who adds foreign hair to her own hair has indeed been dishonest." A wig is artificial hair which resembles the hair of the scalp, and wearing one is dishonesty.'

ii) It is prohibited for the Muslim woman to remove the hair of her eyebrows, completely or partially in any way, including shaving, trimming, or using hair-removing chemicals to remove part of it or all of it. This is because it is the trimming of the eyebrow that the Prophet, may the peace and blessings of Allaah be upon him cursed those who performed it. He cursed the woman who does it for her and the one who has it done for her. This is the changing of the creation of Allah, which Shaytaan swore to order the Sons of Adam to do when he said: as Allaah has mentioned of him:

$$﴿ وَلَأُمُرَنَّهُمْ فَلَيُغَيِّرُنَّ خَلْقَ اللَّهِ ﴾$$

'And I shall order them, and thus they will change the creation of Allaah.' [Al-Nisa: 119].

In a confirmed hadeeth from Ibn Mas'ood, may Allaah be pleased with him, it is narrated that he said: 'Allaah has cursed the tatooist, and the one who is tattooed, the one who has her eyebrows trimmed, and the

24

one who creates gaps between her teeth to increase her beauty, those who seek to alter the creation of Allaah.' Then he said: 'Why should I not curse those whom the Messenger of Allaah, may the peace and blessings of Allaah be upon him cursed this (order) is also in the Book of Allah?' - meaning Allaah's statement:

﴿ وَمَآ ءَاتَىٰكُمُ ٱلرَّسُولُ فَخُذُوهُ وَمَا نَهَىٰكُمْ عَنْهُ فَٱنتَهُواْ ﴾

"Whatever the Messenger has ordered then obey him, and whatever he has forbade then leave it." [Hashr: 7].

Ibn Katheer mentioned this in his Tafseer (2/359, Dar al-Andalus Edition).

Many women today have been affected by this dangerous sickness that is one of the major sins, to such an extent that trimming of the eyebrow has become almost a daily necessity. It is also not permissible for a woman to obey her husband if he orders her to do this, because it is a sin.

iii) It is not permissible for a Muslim woman to create gaps between her teeth to enhance her beauty, by filing her teeth with an iron file to create a small gap between the teeth. However, if the tooth is broken or worm-eaten, and she needs an operation to correct this defect, or they are crooked and she needs to straighten them in order to remove this defect, then no sin is involved, as this is a medical treatment and removal of a defect; and this should be done under the hands of a female specialist doctor.

iv) It is not permissible for a woman to place tattoos on her body, because the Prophet, may the peace and blessings of Allaah be upon him cursed the tattooist and the one tattooed. This action is haraam, and is one of the major sins as the Prophet, may the peace and blessings of Allaah be upon him cursed the one who does it and the one who has it done for her. A curse of the Prophet, may the peace and blessings of Allaah be upon him is only applied in the case of a major sin.

v) The ruling concerning women dyeing their hands and feet with *henna*, and tinting their hair.

1. Dyeing with henna. Imaam Nawawi stated in *al-Majmu'* [1/324]:

> As for dyeing of the hands and feet with henna, it is mustahabb (preferred) for the married woman because of the well-known hadeeths regarding it.

He is referring to what has been narrated by Abu Dawud that a woman asked 'A'isha, may Allaah be pleased with her, may Allaah be pleased with her concerning dying with henna and she replied, 'There is no harm, but I dislike it because my beloved, the Messenger of Allaah, may the peace and blessings of Allaah be upon him, used to dislike its smell.' It has been narrated by Nasaa'i that she said: 'A woman once stretched out her hand from behind a veil to give a note to the Messenger of Allaah, may the peace and blessings of Allaah be upon him. The Prophet, may the peace and blessings of Allaah be upon him withheld his hand and said: "I do not know, is this the hand of a man or of a woman?" She said: "It is the hand of a woman." He said: "If it was the hand of a woman, you would dye your nails (meaning with henna).'" Narrated by Abu Dawud and Nasaa'i. However, she should not paint her nails with substances which solidify and prevent water from touching them, thus stopping her from making ritual purification (wudhoo).

2. As regards a woman dyeing her hair, if it is gray, then she may do so as long as she does not dye it black, because of the general prohibition by the Prophet, may the peace and blessings of Allaah be upon him of dyeing the hair black. Imaam Nawawi stated in *Riyadh As-Saaliheen* (p. 626):

> The Chapter On The Prohibition Of A Man And A Woman Of Dyeing Their Hair Black.

He also stated in *al-Majmu'* [1/324]:

> There is no difference between a man and a woman regarding the prohibition of dyeing with black, and this is our madhhab (juristic school of thought)."

However if the hair is black, then for her to change it to another colour, then my opinion is that this is not permissible as there is no need for it, since the blackness of hair is a sign of beauty and not a defect which needs to be changed. Another reason is that this is a form of imitating the disbelieving women.

3. It is permissible for a woman to wear gold and silver jewellery, as is the custom, and this is by the consensus of the scholars. However, it is not permissible for her to display this jewellery in front of men she could

27

conceivably marry (i.e. non-mahrams); instead she should cover it, particularly when she leaves her house and is exposed to the view of men as this creates fitna (corruption). A woman is prohibited from allowing men to hear the sound of her ankle bracelets, which are worn under the clothes; what do you think will be the judgement concerning jewellery that is clearly visible?

Chapter 3

Laws Regarding Menstruation, False Menstruation & Lochia

1. Menstruation and laws pertaining to it

In the Shari'ah, menstruation is defined as the blood that comes out of the lower part of the womb of a woman at regular intervals naturally, and without any sickness or injury. It is a natural occurrence that Allaah has created the daughters of Adam to experience. Allaah created it for the benefit of the child while it is in the womb, and made it turn into milk in its mother after its birth. Thus, if the woman is not pregnant or nursing a child, this blood remains without use, and so it is discharged at regular intervals. These periods are normally referred to as 'the custom' or 'the monthly cycle'.

The age at which a Woman starts menstruating

Usually, the youngest age at which it is possible for a female to start menstruating is nine years of age, and she may continue to menstruate until she is fifty. Allaah says:

﴿ وَٱلَّٰٓـِٔى يَئِسۡنَ مِنَ ٱلۡمَحِيضِ مِن نِّسَآئِكُمۡ إِنِ ٱرۡتَبۡتُمۡ فَعِدَّتُهُنَّ ثَلَٰثَةُ أَشۡهُرٖ وَٱلَّٰٓـِٔى لَمۡ يَحِضۡنَ ﴾

"And those of your women as have passed the age of monthly courses, for them the prescribed period ('*Iddah*), if you have any doubts (about their periods) is three months; and for those who have no courses (their prescribed periods is three months likewise)." [Al-Talaq: 4]

Those who have passed the age of menstruation are those women who have reached the age of fifty, while those who have no courses are those who are young and not up to the age of nine.

Laws pertaining to the woman in menses

1. It is haraam to have sexual intercourse with a woman while she is menstruating. Allaah says:

﴿ وَيَسۡـَٔلُونَكَ عَنِ ٱلۡمَحِيضِ قُلۡ هُوَ أَذٗى فَٱعۡتَزِلُواْ ٱلنِّسَآءَ فِى ٱلۡمَحِيضِ وَلَا تَقۡرَبُوهُنَّ حَتَّىٰ يَطۡهُرۡنَ فَإِذَا تَطَهَّرۡنَ

30

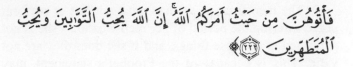

فَأْتُوهُنَّ مِنْ حَيْثُ أَمَرَكُمُ ٱللَّهُ إِنَّ ٱللَّهَ يُحِبُّ ٱلتَّوَّٰبِينَ وَيُحِبُّ ٱلْمُتَطَهِّرِينَ ﴿٢٢٢﴾

"They ask you concerning menstruation. Say it is filth, so keep away from women during their menses, and do not go unto them until they are clean (from menses). And when they have purified themselves, then approach them as Allaah has ordained for you (approach them in any manner as long as it is in the vagina). Allaah loves those who turn unto Him in repentance, and loves those who purify and clean themselves." [Al-Baqara: 222]

This prohibition continues until the blood of the menstruation stops and she takes her ritual bath. Allaah says:

﴿ وَلَا تَقْرَبُوهُنَّ حَتَّىٰ يَطْهُرْنَ فَإِذَا تَطَهَّرْنَ فَأْتُوهُنَّ مِنْ حَيْثُ أَمَرَكُمُ ٱللَّهُ ﴾

"And do not go unto them until they are clean (from menses). And when they have purified themselves, then approach them as Allaah has ordained for you."

It is permissible for her husband to have sexual pleasure with her as long as he does not have sex with her. This is because of the Prophet's statement, may the peace and blessings of Allaah be upon him, 'Do everything except have sex her.' Narrated by Muslim.

31

2. The menstruating woman must not fast or perform prayers during the period of her menstruation - she is not permitted to do these things, and if she does they are not valid. This is because of the Prophet's statement, may the peace and blessings of Allaah be upon him, 'If a woman menstruates, does she not leave praying and fasting?' Narrated by Bukhaari and Muslim. Once the woman has finished her period and has purified herself, she must make up the days of fasting that she missed, although she does not make up her prayer. This is proved by the statement of A'isha, may Allaah be pleased with her, 'When we used to menstruate during the time of the Messenger of Allaah, may the peace and blessings of Allaah be upon him, we were ordered to make up our fasts and we were not ordered to make up our prayers.' Narrated by Bukhaari and Muslim. The difference between the two, and Allaah knows best, is that the prayer is performed frequently; the woman would face difficulty and hardships if she had to make up the prayers she missed, unlike fasting which is obligatory less frequently.

3. The menstruating woman is not permitted to touch the Qur'aan, unless it has a cover on it. Allaah says:

﴿ لَا يَمَسُّهُۥ إِلَّا ٱلۡمُطَهَّرُونَ ﴾

"Which (the Qur'an) none can touch but the purified ones." [Al-Waqi'ah: 79]

Also in the letter the Messenger of Allaah, may the peace and blessings of Allaah be upon him wrote to

'Amru ibn Hazam, may Allaah be pleased with him: 'No one should touch the Mushaf (the Qur'aan) unless they be in a state of ritual purity.' Narrated by Nasaa'i and others, and this hadeeth is almost a mutwaatir hadeeth (a hadeeth with so many chains of narration that it could not possibly be untrue) because of the number of scholars who accepted it as a proof. Ibn Taymiyyah said: 'The madhhab (juristic schools) of the four Imaams is that none should touch the Mushaf unless they are in a state of ritual purity.' As for the ruling regarding reading the Qur'aan without touching the Mushaf, the Scholars have differed, although the safest opinion is that she should not read the Qur'aan unless it be out of necessity -for example, if she fears that she will forget some verses, and Allaah knows best.

4. It is haraam for the menstruating woman to perform tawaaf round the House of Allaah (the Ka'ba). This is proven by the statement of the Prophet, may the peace and blessings of Allaah be upon him to A'isha, may Allaah be pleased with her, 'Do everything the pilgrim does, but do not perform tawaaf of the House until you have purified yourself." Narrated by Bukhaari and Muslim.

5. It is haraam for the menstruating woman to stay in the Masjid. The statement of the Prophet, may the peace and blessings of Allaah be upon him, proves this: 'Surely, I do not permit the Masjid for the menstruating woman or the one who is in janaba (unclean from sexual intercourse).' Narrated by Abu Dawud. As well as statement of the Prophet, may the peace and blessings of

Allaah be upon him: 'Surely, the Masjid is not permissible for the menstruating woman or the one who is unclean.' Narrated by Ibn Maajah. It is permissible for her to pass through the Masjid, because of the hadeeth of A'isha, may Allaah be pleased with her when she said: 'The Messenger of Allah said: "Give me the mat which is in the Masjid, " So I replied, "I am menstruating." He said: "Your menstruation is not in your hand."' The author of *al-Muntaqaa* stated, 'This was narrated by a group of Scholars except Bukhaari [1/140].'

There is no harm if a menstruating woman pronounces Islaamic invocations, including the glorification of Allaah, praise of Allaah, and supplication, or to regularly pronounce the authentic supplications of the morning and evening, and before going to sleep and when waking up. There is also no harm if she reads books of Islamic knowledge, including Tafseer, Hadeeth and Fiqh.

Note: Regarding yellowish and brownish discharges

If during the normal period, yellowish or brownish discharges occur, the woman must consider these as part of her menstruation, and thus the previous laws apply to them. If these discharges occur outside her normal period, then she should not consider them to be menstruation, and should instead consider herself to still be in a state of purity. The statement of Umm 'Atiyya, may Allaah be pleased with her: 'After our menstruation, we never used to consider the yellowish or

34

brownish discharges as being anything,' proves this. Abu Dawud narrated this, and Bukhaari narrated this hadeeth without the words: 'After our menstruation.' This hadeeth has been considered by the scholars of hadeeth to have the same import as a direct statement of the Prophet, may the peace and blessings of Allaah be upon him, at it implies the acknowledgement of the Prophet, may the peace and blessings of Allaah be upon him. The inverse of this hadeeth indicates that these discharges, if they occur before the end of the menstruation, are treated in the same way as normal menstruation.

Note: How does a woman know that her menstruation has ended?

The end of the menstruation is signified by the cessation of the flow of blood, which can be recognised in two ways:

i) The flow of a white discharge. This is a white dicharge resembling whitewash, and it normally flows after the menstruation. It's colour changes according to the differences in the conditions of women.

ii) The drying of the vagina. She finds that out by inserting a piece of cotton into her private part, and it comes out dry – without any sign of blood, or yellowish or brownish discharge.

What the woman must do at the end of her menses

At the end of her menstruation the woman must perform a ritual cleansing – which involves washing her entire body with the intention of purifying herself. This is proved by the Prophet's statement, may the peace and blessings of Allaah be upon him: 'And if your menstruation occurs then leave prayer, and when it ends, wash yourself and resume praying.' Narrated by Bukhaari.

The method of this cleansing (Ghusl):

The woman makes the intention of removing the impurity, or purifying herself to perform the prayer and similar acts of worship. Then she should say, 'Bismillah' (in the name of Allaah). She should then pour water over her entire body, and wet the roots of her hair with it, although if she has it tied, it is not necessary to undo it; she merely wets it with the water. It is also permissible if she uses Sidr (the leaves of the lotus tree) or some other form of cleansing agent. It is also mustahab (preferred) for her to use a piece of cotton scented with musk or other perfume to apply to her vagina after washing. This is proved by the order the Prophet, may the peace and blessings of Allaah be upon him gave to Asmaa to do so. Narrated by Muslim.

Important Note

If the menstruating woman or the woman with lochia (bleeding after childbirth) becomes pure from the bleeding before the setting of the sun, then she must pray the Dhuhr and Asr prayers of that day. If she becomes pure before the Fajr prayer, then she should pray the Maghrib and Esha prayers of that night. This is because the time allowed for the latter prayers (i.e. Asr and Esha), is also a time allowed for the former prayers (i.e. Dhuhr and Magrib) in times of necessity (a similar case being during travel).

Shaykh al-Islaam Ibn Taymiyyah stated in *al-Fataawa* [22/434]:

> Due to this, the majority of the scholars such as Maalik, Shaafi'i and Ahmad were of the opinion that if a woman becomes pure from her menses at the end of the day, then she must pray both Dhuhr and Asr. If she becomes pure at the end of the night, she must pray both Magrib and Esha. This has been conveyed from Abd ar-Rahmaan Ibn Awf, Abu Hurayrah and Ibn Abbaas, and the reason for this is that the times for both prayers is combined in times of necessity; so if she becomes pure at the end of the day, then the time of Dhuhr in her case still remains and so she must pray it before Asr. If she becomes pure at the end of the night then the time of Magrib for her still remains, so she must pray it before Esha.

If the time of prayer comes, and she menstruates or starts discharging lochia after childbirth before she is able to pray, then the strongest opinion is that she does not have to make up that prayer. Shaykh al-Islaam Ibn Taymiyyah stated in *Majmu' al-Fataawa* [23/335] regarding this issue:

> The best proofs are the juristic conclusion of Abu Haneefah and Maalik: that she does not have to make up any prayers, because to make up a prayer requires a separate specific order (from Allaah) – and there is no such order here for her to make up her prayer. Another reason is that her delay in observing her prayer was for a legitimate reason, therefore she is not guilty of negligence.

> As for the one who oversleeps during a prayer time, or innocently forgets to pray, then this person is also not guilty of negligence. When he does pray that prayer, it is not considered as making up a missed prayer, because the prayer time for that person with regard to that particular prayer starts when they remember or when they awaken.

Istihaadah (False Menstruation)

False menstruation is the flow of blood that occurs at a time outside the normal menstrual cycle, (in the Arabic original 'Blood which flows from a vein known as the 'Aadhil', outside of its normal time.') The woman who is afflicted with this type of bleeding has a problem, because of the strong resemblance between this blood and the normal menstrual blood. If she continues to bleed in this way, or most of the time, then which blood should she consider to be part of her normal menstruation, and which blood should she consider to be due to false menstruation, and thus not leave prayer and fasting? This is because the woman who has this type of bleeding is subject to the same laws as a woman outside her menstrual cycle.

Based on this, the woman who has this type of bleeding can be classified under one of the following groups:

1. A woman who used to have a normal regular menstrual cycle before the onset of this bleeding. For example, prior to this bleeding she may have been menstruating for a period of five days or eight days at the beginning of each month or during the middle of each month. Thus, she knows her normal menstrual cycle. The woman in this case would leave prayer and fasting during her normal menstrual period and be subject to the laws of menstruation. When the menstrual period ends, she would wash herself, and begin to pray normally, and would consider the blood that flows from her after this as being from false menstruation. This is proved by the statement of the Prophet, may the peace and blessings of Allaah be upon him to Umm Habibah, may Allaah be pleased with her: 'Sit (i.e. do not pray) for the length of the period which you used to observe as your normal menstrual period, then take your (ritual) bath and pray.' Narrated by Muslim. Another proof is his statement to Faatima Bint Abu Hubaish, may Allaah be pleased with her: 'Indeed (what you see), is blood flowing from a vein and not menstruation, so when your normal period approaches then leave prayer.' Narrated by Bukhaari and Muslim.

2. If the woman does not have a known regular period, but the blood of her menstruation is distinct from the other blood, for example if it is dark in colour or thick or it has a distinct smell, while the other blood does not have these characteristics, for example it is red, odourless or not thick; then in this case, she will consider blood which has the same characteristics as her normal menstrual blood as menstruation, and thus she will leave prayer and fasting during the period of its flow. She will consider any other blood as false menstruation, and so she will cleanse herself when the blood of her normal menstruation ends. She will then pray and fast, and consider herself to be in a state of purity. This is proved by the statement of the Prophet, may the peace and blessings of Allaah be upon him to Faatima Bint Abu Hubaish, may Allaah be pleased with her: 'If it is the blood of menstruation, then it is well-known because it is dark in colour, and thus you should leave prayer. If it is of the other type, then you must perform wudhoo and pray.' Narrated by Abu Dawud and Nasaa'i, and Ibn Hibbaan and al-Haakim say it is sahih. This hadeeth proves that the woman afflicted with false menstruation should take into consideration the characteristics of the blood, and differentiate between the blood of menstruation and the other type of blood.

3. If the woman does not have a regular period or cannot differentiate between her normal menstrual blood and other types based on the characteristics of the blood, then she must leave prayer for the most common duration of menstruation, which is six or seven days in a

month. This is because it is the normal menstrual period for most women. This is proved by the statement of the Prophet, may the peace and blessings of Allaah be upon him to Hamnah Bint Jahash, may Allaah be pleased with her: 'This (affliction) is (caused by) harm from the Shaytaan, so consider your menstruation to be six or seven days then wash yourself. Then pray for twenty-four or twenty-three days, and fast. This is sufficient for you, so observe this (as your menstruation) just as the rest of the women menstruate.' Narrated by Ahmad, Abu Dawud, Tirmidhi, Nasaa'i and Ibn Maajah, and it was authenticated by Tirmidhi.

Summary

The woman who has a regular cycle should stick to that, and the woman who can differentiate should work with that. The woman without these two qualities must treat her menstruation as being six or seven days. This conclusion combines the accounts of the three different narrations from the Prophet, may the peace and blessings of Allaah be upon him, concerning the woman afflicted with this type of bleeding.

Shaykh al-Islaam Ibn Taymiyyah said:

The signs (by which false menstruation can be judged) that have been mentioned are six: The normal menstrual cycle, which is the strongest indication because it is the normal time for menstruation, and for no other types of blood. The second is by differentiation, because blood that is dark in colour, and is thick, and has an odour is more likely to be menstrual

41

blood than a red blood. The third is by taking into account the normal period of menstruation experienced by most women, because the general rule is to give the individual case the rule of the predominant majority.

These three signs are proved by the Sunnah and through sound analogy.

He then mentioned the rest of the signs that the scholars have mentioned, and finally concluded:

The most correct position is to consider the signs that have been proved by the Sunnah and disregard other than them.

What the woman afflicted with this type of bleeding should do when she is considered to be in a state of purity

1. She must perform the ritual cleansing at the end of her actual menstruation period, as has previously been mentioned.

2. She must wash her private parts at every prayer time, in order to remove from it traces of the blood that has flowed, and must place a piece of cotton in the opening to prevent further seepage, and something over it that will keep it in place (in other words, use a ladies pad with wings). She should then perform wudhoo at the start of each prayer time in order to observe the prayer. The statement of the Prophet, may the peace and blessings of Allaah be upon him, 'Leave the prayer during the days of your menses, and then wash yourself, and make wudhoo for every prayer,' proves this.

Narrated by Abu Dawud, Ibn Maajah and Tirmidhi, who said this hadeeth was hasan (acceptable). The Prophet, may the peace and blessings of Allaah be upon him also said: 'Apply a piece of cotton to cover (i.e. stem the flow of fluid from) the place.' It is also permissible to use the personal hygiene products used today.

The Laws Regarding Lochia (Nifaas)

Nifaas is the Islaamic name given to blood that leaves the womb during and after childbirth. It is the blood that has been withheld during the pregnancy in the womb, and so when the baby is born, the blood seeps out of the womb little by little. The blood that can be seen seeping out of the womb during the first signs of labour before childbirth is also nifaas. The scholars restrict it to what is seen two or three days before childbirth. Normally, this blood begins to appear during the actual childbirth. Actual childbirth is considered to be when a form resembling a human being is delivered. The least amount of time after which a foetus is recognisable as having a human form is eighty-one days, and more commonly three months. If any miscarriage occurs before this time, and bleeding occurs with it, then the woman must not pay any attention to this blood and should continue to pray and fast, as this is bad blood and is caused by bleeding, and thus it carries the same judgement as false menstrual blood.

Normally, the longest duration of nifaas is forty days, starting at childbirth or two or three days before it, as has been mentioned. This is proved by the statement of Umm Salama, may Allaah be pleased with her: 'During the time of the Messenger of Allaah, may the peace and blessings of Allaah be upon him, the women with nifaas would sit (i.e. leave prayer and fasting) for forty days.' Narrated by Tirmidhi.

The scholars have a consensus on this point, as stated by Tirmidhi and others. Before the end of this period, if she becomes pure, that is, blood stops flowing, then she should wash herself and pray, because there is no minimum limit for nifaas, as none has been found in the Sunnah. If the forty days pass and the blood continues to flow, and it corresponds to her normal menstrual period, then the blood is treated as menstrual blood. If however, it does not correspond to one of her periods, then the blood is considered to be false menstruation, and as such she should not leave any prayers or fasting at the end of the forty days. If the blood still flows after forty days, and it does not continue, nor correspond to a menstrual period, in such a situation there are differences of opinions among the scholars.

Rulings pertaining to Nifaas

The laws pertaining to Nifaas are similar to the laws of menstruation in the following ways:

1. It is not permissible to have sexual intercourse with a woman during her nifaas in the same way that it is not

allowed to have intercourse with a menstruating woman. Love-play that does not involve actual intercourse is permissible.

2. It is not permissible for the woman in nifaas to fast, perform prayers, or perform tawaaf around the House, just as is the case for the menstruating woman.

3. It is not permissible for the woman in nifaas to touch the Mushaf while she is in nifaas, or read the Qur'an, as long as she is not in fear of forgetting the Qur'an, as is the case for the menstruating woman.

4. It is obligatory upon the woman in nifaas to make up fasts she missed while in nifaas, just as the menstruating woman must do.

5. The woman must cleanse herself at the end of her nifaas in the same way that it is obligatory on the menstruating woman.

The proofs of these points include:

It is narrated from Umm Salama, may Allaah be pleased with her that she said: 'During the time of the Messenger of Allaah, may the peace and blessings of Allaah be upon him the women in nifaas would sit (i.e. not pray or fast) for forty days.' Narrated by the five scholars except Nasaa'i.

Al-Majd, Ibn Taymiyyah[4] stated in *al-Muntaqaa* [1/184]:

The meaning of the hadeeth is that they were ordered (by the Messenger of Allaah, may the peace and blessings of Allaah be upon him) to sit for forty days, in order that this information not to be considered false (not that all women had a period of nifaas of exactly forty days), because it is not possible that all women of a particular time had the same duration of nifaas or menstruation.

It is narrated from Umm Salama, may Allaah be pleased with her that she said: 'If one of the wives of the Prophet, may the peace and blessings of Allaah be upon him was in her nifaas she would sit for forty days, during which he would not order her to make up her prayers.' Narrated by Abu Dawud.

Note

If the woman was to stop bleeding before the end of the forty days, and she cleansed herself and began to pray and fast, and then the bleeding commenced again, before she has completed the forty days, then the most correct conclusion in this case is that the blood is considered nifaas, and she must leave prayer and fasting. The fasting she observed during the interval is acceptable and she does not have to make it up. See

---

4 Al-Majd Ibn Taymiyyah was the grandfather of Shaykh al-Islaam Ibn Taymiyyah. He was the author of *al-Muntaqaa* of which Imaam Shawkaanee wrote a commentary, *Nayl al-Awtar*.

Majmu' al-Fataawaa by Shaykh Muhammad Ibn Ibrahim [2/102], and the Fataawa of Shaykh Abdul Aziz Ibn Baaz printed by Majallat ad-Da'wa [1/44], and *Hashiyyat Ibn Qaasim 'ala Sharh az-Zaad* [1/405], and the Natural Blood of Women [pp. 55-56], and *Fatwaawa as-Sa'diyyah* [p. 137].

Another Note

Shaykh Abd ar-Rahmaan Ibn Sa'di said:

It becomes clear from what has preceded that the blood of nifaas is caused by childbirth, and that the blood of false menstruation is a symptom of a sickness or something of that nature; but the blood of menstruation is natural and Allah knows best.

See *Kitaab al-Irshaad ulil al-Basaa'ir wa al-Albaab* [p. 24].

The usage of pills

There is no harm if the woman uses pills to stop the flow of menstrual blood if it will not harm her health. Therefore, if she were to use these pills and the menstruation stopped, then she would pray and fast and make tawaaf and these acts would be acceptable from her, as they would be from women in a state of purity.

The Ruling concerning Abortion

You are entrusted, dear Muslim woman by the Shari'ah with what Allaah has created in your womb

47

during pregnancy, and thus you must not attempt to conceal it. Allaah says:

$$ \text{﴿ وَلَا يَحِلُّ لَهُنَّ أَن يَكْتُمْنَ مَا خَلَقَ ٱللَّهُ فِىٓ أَرْحَامِهِنَّ إِن كُنَّ يُؤْمِنَّ بِٱللَّهِ وَٱلْيَوْمِ ٱلْأَخِرِ ﴾} $$

"And it is not lawful for them to conceal what Allah has created in their wombs, if they believe in Allah and the Last Day." [Al-Baqarah: 228]

You should not attempt to force an abortion and terminate the pregnancy in any way, as Allaah has permitted you to eat during the month of Ramadhaan if fasting would be a hardship upon you during your pregnancy, or if it would harm the foetus. Indeed, the operations to perform abortions that have become prevalent in this time are haraam. If the unborn foetus has had its soul breathed into it, and then dies because of an abortion, this constitutes the murder of an individual whose life Allaah has forbidden to be taken except by legitimate right. In this situation, the laws concerning criminal responsibility, in terms of the obligatory payment of blood money according to the juristic details regarding its specific amount are applicable. In addition some scholars have also stated that the obligation of expiation is also applicable here, which is to set free a Muslim slave, and for those who cannot afford it, they would fast for two consecutive months. Some scholars have called this action a lesser form of burying the newborn alive (a practice forbidden by the Qur'an).

Shaykh Muhammad Ibn Ibrahim stated in *Majmu' al-Fataawa*:

Regarding attempts to terminate the pregnancy; this is not permissible unless it has been proved the unborn foetus is already dead. If this is proved then there is no harm.

In the ruling of the Council of the Eminent Scholars (no. 140, dated 20/6/1407), it is stated that:

1. It is not permissible to terminate the pregnancy at any stage except in extremely limited circumstances justified by the Shari'ah.

2. If the pregnancy is in the first stage, which is during the first forty days, and termination during this period would be for an Islamically justified reason, or to avoid some type of harm, the termination is permissible. As for terminating the pregnancy during this period due to the fear of bringing up a child, or out of fear of being unable to provide financially for the child's upbringing and education, or out of fear for their future or because the parents are contented with the number of children they already have, then abortion in this case is not permissible.

3. It is not permissible to terminate the pregnancy if the foetus has developed into a leech-like clot or piece of flesh, until a panel of trusted, qualified doctors has established that the continuation of the pregnancy constitutes a danger to the safety of its mother. For example, if it is feared that she might die. In this case a termination is permissible, after all possible efforts and methods have been employed to avoid this danger.

4. After the third stage of the pregnancy, and after completing four full months of the pregnancy, it is not

permissible to perform an abortion until a panel of trusted specialist doctors have established that the continued presence of the foetus in its' mother's womb will cause her death. This would be after all possible efforts and means have been employed to avert such a situation occurring. The termination under these conditions would be permissible, as it would be warding off the greater of two evils, and procuring the greater of two benefits. The Council in giving this ruling exhorts all to fear Allaah, and to be firm in ascertaining the truth regarding this issue. May Allaah grants all success, and blessings and peace be upon our Prophet, Muhammad, his family and companions.

In the treatise, *The Natural Blood of Women*, by Shaykh Muhammad Saalih Ibn Uthaymeen [p. 60]:

If the intention behind the termination is to kill the child, and this takes place after the soul has been breathed into it, then this act is haraam without any doubt whatsoever, as it constitutes killing an individual without legitimate right. The Qur'an, the Sunnah and the consensus of all the Scholars are clear on the prohibition of killing a protected individual.

Imaam Ibn Al-Jawzi stated in *Kitaab Ahkaam an-Nisaa* [pp. 108-109]:

As the intention behind marriage is the production of children, and as not every drop of semen produces a child, if a child is created then the intention behind the marriage has been fulfilled. Thus, actively seeking to abort the pregnancy is not in accordance with the wisdom behind the marriage. If this occurs in the first stage of the pregnancy, before the soul is breathed into the foetus, then it is a grave sin, as it stops the development of the foetus into perfection. However, this sin is less than aborting a foetus which has had the soul breathed into it. If a deliberate abortion of a foetus that has a soul takes place, it is the same as the murder of a believer. Allaah has said:

$$ \{ \text{وَإِذَا الْمَوْءُودَةُ سُئِلَتْ} \; ⑧ \; \text{بِأَيِّ ذَنبٍ قُتِلَتْ} \; ⑨ \} $$

"And when the female (infant) buried alive is questioned; for what crime she was killed". [Al-Takwir: 8-9]

So dear Muslim woman! You should fear Allaah, and do not seek to commit this terrible sin, for any reason, and do not be misled by deceptive propaganda, and deviate customs that are not based on sound thinking or religion.

Chapter 4

Laws Pertaining To Dressing & Hijaab

A description of the Islaamic dress of a Woman

1. It is obligatory for the dress of a woman to be sufficiently loose and wide to cover her whole body from the sight of men who are not close relatives to her (i.e. those to whom she could get married, according to the Shari'ah). She should not expose to her mahrams (male relatives whom she is not allowed to marry) except those parts of her body that are normally exposed according to custom: her face, hands and feet.

2. The clothes must conceal the shape of her body, and not be transparent, so that the colour and details of her body are exposed.

3. The clothes must be loose fitting, and must not cling to her limbs. In *Saheeh Muslim*, Allaah's Messenger, may the peace and blessings of Allaah be upon him said: 'There are two types of the denizens of hell whom I have not seen. Women who are dressed but appear to be naked, who would be inclined (to evil) and make others incline towards it. Their heads would be

like the humps of the *bukht* (healthy, fat) camel - (inclined to one side or with their hair in a single bun). They will not enter Paradise and they would not smell its odour. And men with whips like the tails of bulls with which they beat the servants of Allaah.'

Ibn Taymiyyah stated in *Majmu' al-Fataawa* [22/146]:

His statement: '...who would be dressed but appear to be naked', means that she would wear clothes that would not conceal her. For example a woman who wears a thin robe which reveals the lines of her body such as her forearms and buttocks, etc. Instead the clothing of a woman should cover her totally and not reveal her body or her proportions, by virtue of its being thick and loose fitting.

4. The woman must not resemble men in her dress. The Prophet, may the peace and blessings of Allaah be upon him cursed the women who resemble men and cursed the men who resemble women. The woman would resemble men in her dress by wearing what is specifically recognised as men's clothes in the society in which she lives. Ibn Taymiyyah said in *Majmu' al-Fataawa* [22/148-149/155]:

So the distinguishing factor between men's clothes and women's goes back to what is appropriate for men and what is appropriate for women. This is defined by what men have been ordered to wear and by what women have been ordered to wear. As for women, they have been ordered to cover themselves and wear Hijaab, and not expose themselves and make a dazzling display of their beauty. Because of this, it is not permissible for a woman to raise her voice to pronounce the Adhaan or Talbiyyah; she is not allowed to ascend Safaa or Marwa; she does not disrobe herself of her undergarments in Ihraam the way that men do. Men have been ordered to expose their heads (in Ihraam) and not wear clothes that are designed to fit the shape of the body; for example, a man should not wear a shirt, trousers, jacket or leather socks...

...and as for a woman, she has not been prohibited from wearing any type of clothes, as she has been ordered to cover and wear Hijaab, and therefore she could not be ordered to do the opposite. However, she is not permitted to cover her face, or wear gloves because these two types of clothing are designed to fit the shape of the body and she has no need of them.'

Then he mentioned that she should cover her face with something other than the Niqaab in the presence of men. He then went on to state finally:

Therefore, if it is apparent that there must be a distinction between men's clothing and women's clothing, which differentiates men from women, and that the clothes of women must be sufficient to cover them; and to the extent that this distinction becomes clear, then the basic ruling regarding this area becomes clear, and it becomes apparent that if certain types of clothes are normally worn by men, then a woman is prohibited from wearing them...

...and if a particular type of cloth is insufficient in covering the woman and also resembles the clothing of men, she is prohibited from wearing it based on both counts of prohibition, and Allah knows best.

5. The woman's clothing must not be attractive to the extent that it attracts gazes when she goes outside, so that she avoids becoming an exhibitionist.

The Hijaab

The meaning of the term 'Hijaab' is that a woman conceals her body from the sight of men who are not mahrams to her. Allaah says:

﴿ وَلَا يُبْدِينَ زِينَتَهُنَّ إِلَّا مَا ظَهَرَ مِنْهَا وَلْيَضْرِبْنَ بِخُمُرِهِنَّ عَلَى جُيُوبِهِنَّ وَلَا يُبْدِينَ زِينَتَهُنَّ إِلَّا لِبُعُولَتِهِنَّ أَوْ ءَابَائِهِنَّ أَوْ ءَابَاءِ بُعُولَتِهِنَّ أَوْ أَبْنَائِهِنَّ أَوْ أَبْنَاءِ بُعُولَتِهِنَّ أَوْ إِخْوَانِهِنَّ ﴾

"And they should not display their adornment except what is apparent thereof; and they should draw their veils over their bosoms, and not display their adornment except to their husbands, or their fathers, or their husbands' fathers, or their sons, or their husbands' sons, or their brothers." [An-Nur: 31]

And He also said:

﴿ وَإِذَا سَأَلْتُمُوهُنَّ مَتَاعًا فَسْأَلُوهُنَّ مِن وَرَاءِ حِجَابٍ ﴾

"And when you ask (the Prophet's wives) for anything you want, ask them from behind a screen" [Al-Ahzab: 53]

The meaning of 'Hijaab' in this verse is any object that conceals a woman such as a wall, a door, or clothes. The verse, even though it was revealed concerning the wives of the Prophet, may the peace and blessings of Allaah be upon him, it's ruling generally encompasses all Muslim women. This is because the wisdom behind the ruling is specified in Allaah's statement:

$$\text{﴿ ذَٰلِكُمْ أَطْهَرُ لِقُلُوبِكُمْ وَقُلُوبِهِنَّ ﴾}$$

"That makes for greater purity for your hearts and theirs." [Al-Ahzab: 53]

This wisdom is general among all men and women. Therefore, the generality of the wisdom also indicates the general applicability of the ruling. Allaah says:

$$\text{﴿ يَٰٓأَيُّهَا ٱلنَّبِيُّ قُل لِّأَزْوَٰجِكَ وَبَنَاتِكَ وَنِسَاءِ ٱلْمُؤْمِنِينَ يُدْنِينَ عَلَيْهِنَّ مِن جَلَٰبِيبِهِنَّ ﴾}$$

"O Prophet! Tell your wives and your daughters and the women of the believers to draw their cloaks (veils) all over their bodies." [Al-Ahzab: 59]

Ibn Taymiyyah stated in *Majmu' al-Fataawa* [22/110-111]:

The Jilbaab is a cover, and Ibn Mas'ood, may Allaah be pleased with him and others called it a 'Ridaa' and the common people (of today) call it 'Izaar'. It is large and covers a woman's head and the rest of her body. Abu 'Ubaydah and others stated that it should hang from the top of her head, the only thing visible being her eyes. The Niqaab is a similar type of clothing.

Among the proof contained in the Sunnah of the Prophet, may the peace and blessings of Allaah be upon him, which indicate the obligation upon the woman to cover her face in front of strangers (like those she could conceivably marry like her male cousins), is the hadeeth of 'A'isha, may Allaah be pleased with her who said: 'Riders used to pass by us when we accompanied the Messenger of Allaah, may the peace and blessings of Allaah be upon him while we were in the state of Ihraam. If they came close to us, we would lower the Jilbaab from our heads onto our faces. When they passed us, we would uncover (our faces).' Narrated by Ahmad, Abu Dawud, and Ibn Maajah. There is a lot of evidence to prove the obligation on the woman to cover her face while in the presence of strangers in the Qur'an and the Sunnah. I refer the Muslim Sister to the treatise regarding Hijaab, clothing and prayer, by Ibn Taymiyyah, and the treatise on Hijaab by Shaykh Abd al-Azeez ibn Abdullah ibn Baaz and the book *Risaalat As-Saarim al-Mashoor 'Ala al-Muftooneenah Bi-'Sufoor* by Shaykh Hamood ibn Abdullah At-Tuwayjari and *Risaalat al-Hijaab* by Shaykh Muhammad ibn Saalih al-'Uthaymeen. These treatises contain ample information concerning this point.

The Muslim sister should be aware that those scholars who ruled that it is permissible for her to show her face, in addition to the fact that their conclusion is weak, have stipulated the condition that there should not be any fitna (temptation caused by uncovering her face). Fitna is unavoidable, particularly in these times when men and women are less religious, and there is little modesty, while at the same time the promoters of fitna have increased, and women have developed different cosmetics that they apply to their faces causing fitna. Therefore, the Muslim Sister should be warned about this and should adhere to the Hijaab, which by the will of Allaah, will protect her from fitna. None of the recognised Muslim scholars of the past or present, has permitted what these corrupted women have fallen into.

Some Muslim women are hypocritical in their usage of the Hijaab; if they are in a society that adheres to the wearing of Hijaab they wear it, and if they are in a society that does not adhere to the wearing of the Hijaab, they do not. Some of them wear Hijaab in open, public places, whereas if they enter a shop, a hospital, or they are speaking to a jeweller or a women's tailor, they uncover their faces, and arms as if they are with their husband, or one of her mahrams. The women who do this must fear Allaah. We have witnessed some women when coming back from foreign countries do not wear Hijaab until the plane lands at one of the airports of this country (Saudi Arabia). It is as if the Hijaab has become a local custom and not a religious duty.

The Muslim sister should be aware that the Hijaab protects her from evil glances emanating from those who have a sickness in their hearts and the dogs among mankind. The Hijaab also protects her from evil desires so she should adhere and cling to the Hijaab and not be persuaded or tempted by media that opposes the Hijaab or belittles its significance, as those who spread this media only desire evil for her. Allaah says:

﴿ وَيُرِيدُ ٱلَّذِينَ يَتَّبِعُونَ ٱلشَّهَوَٰتِ أَن تَمِيلُواْ مَيْلًا عَظِيمًا ﴾

"But the wish of those who follow their lusts is that you should deviate away (from the Right path), - far, far away." [An-Nisa: 27]

Chapter 5

Laws Pertaining To The Woman Regarding Her Salaat

It is obligatory on the Muslim woman to observe her Salaat (regular prayers) at the appointed time, fulfilling all its conditions, fundamental actions and obligatory practices. Allah has said to the Mothers of the Believers, may Allaah be pleased with them (the wives of the Prophet, may the peace and blessings of Allaah be upon him):

﴿ وَأَقِمْنَ ٱلصَّلَوٰةَ وَءَاتِينَ ٱلزَّكَوٰةَ وَأَطِعْنَ ٱللَّهَ وَرَسُولَهُۥٓ ﴾

"And establish the salat (regular prayers) and give the zakat, and obey Allaah and His Messenger." [Al-Ahzab: 33]

This order applies to Muslim women in general.

Salaat is the second pillar of Islaam and is the basis and foundation of Islaam. To leave the Salaat is an act of disbelief that takes a person out of Islaam (apostasy). There is no status of religion or Islaam for one who does not pray - be he a man or a woman. To delay the prayer without a legitimate reason is a way of neglecting the prayer. Allaah says:

$$\langle\!\langle \text{ فَخَلَفَ مِنْ بَعْدِهِمْ خَلْفٌ أَضَاعُوا الصَّلَاةَ وَاتَّبَعُوا الشَّهَوَاتِ فَسَوْفَ } \rangle\!\rangle$$

$$\text{ يَلْقَوْنَ غَيًّا ۝ إِلَّا مَن تَابَ } \rangle\!\rangle$$

"But after them there followed a posterity who neglected prayers and followed lusts. Soon then will they be thrown in Hell. Except those who repent ..." [Maryam: 59, 60]

In his Tafseer (Explanation of the Qur'an), Ibn Katheer quoted from a number of the Commentators of the Qur'aan that the meaning of 'neglecting Salaat' is to miss their appointed times by praying after the appointed times have expired, and the meaning of 'al-Ghay' which they will meet, is 'a great loss'. This word has also been said to mean the name of a ravine in Hell.

Women also have certain rulings, which are specific to them concerning their prayer, which are as follows:

1. Women do not have to announce the Adhaan or the Iqaama. The reason for this is that the Adhaan and the Iqaama were decreed for those for whom raising the voice was permissible - and this does not include women. Therefore, it is not permissible for the woman to raise her voice and announce the Adhaan or the Iqaama. In *al-Mughni* [2/68]:

> We are not aware of any disagreement regarding this point.

2. The woman's entire body must be covered during the prayer except for her face, although there is a

longstanding disagreement among the scholars regarding her palms and feet. This applies when she is in the company of those who are related to her in a way that prohibits marriage between them (i.e. mahrams, for example, her father, uncle or brother). If she is in a place where other men would see her then she must cover herself fully, as she would cover herself outside of prayer. Therefore, she must cover her head her neck and the rest of her body down to the level of her feet. The Prophet, may the peace and blessings of Allaah be upon him said: 'The Salaat of a woman who has reached the age of menstruation will not be accepted unless she is wearing a Khimaar.' Narrated by The Five scholars. The Khimaar covers the head and the neck. Umm Salama, may Allaah be pleased with her narrated that she asked the Prophet, may the peace and blessings of Allaah be upon him, 'Should the woman pray if she is wearing only a chemise and a Khimaar without wearing an Izaar (similar to a skirt)? He said: "(Yes), if the chemise or tunic is long and flows down to cover the top of her feet.' Reported by Abu Dawud and the scholars asserted that this hadeeth is mawqoof (it is actually a statement of Umm Salama, may Allaah be pleased with her, and not that of the Prophet, may the peace and blessings of Allaah be upon him). These two hadeeth indicate that it is obligatory for her to cover her head and her neck, as in the hadeeth of A'ishah, may Allaah be pleased with her, and the hadeeth of Umm Salama, may Allaah be pleased with her indicates that she must also cover the rest of her body down to the top of her feet. By the consensus of the Scholars, it is permissible for her to uncover her face where no strangers will see her. Shaykh Al-Islaam, Ibn Taymiyyah stated in *Majmu' al-Fataawa* [22/113-114]:

If the woman prays on her own she is ordered to wear the Khimaar, and outside Salaat it is permissible to uncover her head inside her house. One of the rights of Allah is that a person dresses decently, and therefore it is not permissible to perform Tawaaf of the Ka'ba unclothed, even alone at night, or pray while being unclothed even when they are alone...

...so there is no link between the obligation of covering oneself in Salaat and being seen by others in any away.

It is stated in *al-Mughni* [2/328]:

As for the rest of the body of a free woman, it is obligatory to cover it during Salaat. If a part of her body becomes uncovered during the Salaat, then the Salaat becomes invalid, unless the uncovered part is very small. This is the position of Maalik, Awzaa'i and Shaafi'i.

3. Mentioned in *al-Mughni* [2/258]:

A woman should gather herself together (i.e. her arms and legs) when she is in rukoo' (bowing) and sujood (prostration) instead of stretching herself out, and she should sit cross-legged or gather her legs together and set them on her right side instead of sitting with her legs underneath her or with one tucked under the other (as the men do when they pray), as the former positions are less revealing.

Imam Nawawi stated in *al-Majmu'* [3/455]:

Shaafi'i stated in *al-Mukhtasar*, 'There is no difference between men and women in the actions of the prayer except that it is preferred that a woman gathers herself together, and that she presses her thighs against her stomach when she makes sujood - as this is the best way to cover her body shape, and I prefer for her to do this while in rukoo' and all other parts of the Salaat.'

4. Congregational prayers for women led by one of them is an issue about which there is disagreement between the scholars. Some permit it and others do not, although the majority say that there is nothing wrong with it, as the Prophet, may the peace and blessings of Allaah be upon him once ordered Umm Warakah, may Allaah be pleased with her to lead the members of her household in prayer. Narrated by Abu Dawud, and Ibn Khuzaymah authenticated this hadeeth. Some scholars say that this action is mustahab or preferred based on this hadeeth, while others regard it as makrooh (disliked), while others allow it in supererogatory prayers but not in obligatory prayers. I feel that the correct opinion is that it is mustahab. For extra details regarding this issue see *al-Mughni* [2/202] and *al-Majmu'* by Imaam Nawawi 94/84-85]. A woman should only recite loudly when there are no men present who she could legally marry.

5. It is permissible for the women to leave their homes and go and pray in the Masjid as the men do, although it is better for them to pray in their houses. Muslim reported in his Saheeh, 'Do no forbid the female servants of Allaah from the houses of Allaah.' He also

said: 'Do not prevent the women from praying in the Masjids, but their houses are better for them.' Reported by Ahmad and Abu Dawud. So it is better for the women to remain in their homes and pray because it is more concealing. If the woman does leave her house to pray in the Masjid, then it is imperative that she complies with the following:

♦ **She should be fully dressed and covered with a Hijaab.** A'ishah, may Allaah be pleased with her said: 'The women used to pray with the Messenger of Allaah, may the peace and blessings of Allaah be upon him, then they would leave wrapped up in their clothes unidentifiable because of the darkness of dawn...' Agreed upon.

♦ **She should not wear perfume**. This is proven by the statement of the Prophet, may the peace and blessings of Allaah be upon him, 'Do not forbid the female servants of Allaah from going to the Masjids of Allaah, and they should go out unperfumed.' Reported by Ahmad and Abu Dawud. Abu Hurairah, may Allah be pleased with him said that, 'The Messenger of Allaah, may the peace and blessings of Allaah be upon him said: "Any woman who has applied perfume must not attend the Esha prayer with us."' Reported by Muslim, Abu Dawud and Nasaa'i. In the hadeeth reported by Muslim from Zaynab, the wife of Ibn Mas'ud, 'If any of you (women) comes to the Masjid then do not apply perfume.'

Imaam Shawkaani said in *Nayl al-Awtaar* [3/140-141]:

This hadeeth proves that it is permissible for women to go to the Masjids as long as it does not involve fitna (flirtation), or involve things that cause fitna such as applying perfume

He also said:

These hadeeth prove that it is permissible for women to go to the Masjids as long as when going they do not wear things which cause fitna, such as perfume, jewellery or any form of adornment.

♦ **She should not go outside dressed provocatively**, wearing beautiful clothes or jewellery. The mother of the believers A'isha, may Allaah be pleased with her said: 'If the Messenger of Allaah, may the peace and blessings of Allaah be upon him had seen what we see happening among the women, he would have forbidden them from going to the Masjid in the same way that the children of Israa'eel forbade their women.' Agreed upon.

Imaam Shawkaani stated in *Nayl-Awtaar* (see previous source) commenting on A'isha's statement, may Allaah be pleased with her: '...if he had seen what we see...':

...meaning the wearing of fine clothes, perfume, adornment, and display of beauty. Instead, (during the Prophet's time, may the peace and blessings of Allaah be upon him) the women used to go out wearing clothes wrapped around their bodies, thick cloaks and veils.

Imaam Ibn al-Jawzee stated in *Kitaab Ahkaam An-Nisaa'* [p. 39]:

It is appropriate that a woman be warned from going out whatever the circumstance, even if she feels safe, as the people may not be safe from her. If it becomes absolutely necessary for her to go out, she must do so only with the permission of her husband, and with a decent appearance, and she must stay clear of busy streets and markets, taking care that her voice is not heard. She must walk along the side of the street and not in the middle.

Az-Zuhree says, regarding the action of the Prophet, may the peace and blessings of Allaah be upon him, of delaying his leaving his praying place after prayer: 'In our opinion, the action of the Prophet, may the peace and blessings of Allaah be upon him, of remaining in his praying place a little after the salaam, and Allah knows best, is in order that the women are able to depart from the Masjid (before the men start leaving).' [*Fath al-Baari* 2/334-335)]. Narrated by Bukhaari. See also *as-Sharh al-Kabeer 'ala al-Muqni* [1/422].

Imaam Shawkaani stated in *Nayl-al-Awtaar* [2/326]:

The hadeeth proves that it is mustahab for the Imaam to take into account the state of the people who pray behind him, and to take precautions to avoid what might lead to sin, and to avoid situations which might lead to suspicions; and it also shows the unacceptability of free-mixing between men and women in the streets, let alone the houses.

Imaam Nawawi stated in *al-Majmu'* [3/455]:

Women differ from men with regard to congregational prayer in several ways:

It is not as obligatory upon women to attend as it is upon men.

(If a woman leads other women in prayer) she who leads the prayer does not stand in front of those who pray with her, instead she stands in the middle.

It is enough for a single woman to pray behind a single man, and not by his side – which is different from the situation for men.

If they pray in rows behind men, then the last row of women is better than the first row of women.

From what has preceded, the prohibition of mixing between men and women is clear.

6. Women going to 'Eid Salaat. Umm 'Atiyyah, may Allaah be pleased with her said: 'The Messenger of Allaah, may the peace and blessings of Allaah be upon him ordered the elderly women, the menstruating women and the young virgins who normally stayed indoors to attend the prayer for Eid al-Fitr and al-Adhaa. As for the menstruating women, they were to distance themselves from the Salaat (in another narration, 'the place of prayer'), and they were to attend the festivities and the prayers of the Muslims.' Narrated by the six Scholars of Hadeeth. Imaam Shawkaani stated [3/306]:

This hadeeth and others with the same meaning prove the legality of women attending the congregational prayers on the two 'Eids, without any distinction between virgins or non-virgins, young or old women, those in their menstrual periods, and others as long as

68

she is not in her 'Iddah (post-divorce period of seclusion) or that by going out she will cause fitna, or she has some other excuse...

Ibn Taymiyyah stated in *Majmu' al-Fataawa* [6/458-459]:

So he, may Allaah bless him and grant him peace, informed the believing women that praying in their homes was better for them than attending Jum'ah prayers and congregational prayers; except the 'Eid prayers, which he has ordered them to attend. He ordered them to attend the Eid prayers, and Allaah knows best, for the following reasons:

It occurs twice in a year so it is acceptable, unlike Jum'ah and the congregational prayers.

There is no substitute for this prayer, unlike Jum'ah and the congregational prayers as she can pray Dhuhr in her house and it is considered her Jum'ah prayer.

It usually involves going out to an open place (or some other such place), to make remembrance of Allaah and it is therefore similar to Hajj in certain aspects, and for this reason the greater of the two 'Eids is in the Hajj season in accordance with the pilgrimage of the pilgrims.

The Shaafi'i madhhab has placed a condition on the type of women who are allowed to go to 'Eid prayer. They must not be of outstanding social status. Imaam Nawawi stated in *al-Majmu'* [5/13]:

Shaafi'i and his companions said: 'It is mustahabb for the women who are not of an outstanding social status to attend the 'Eid prayer. As for those who have such a status, their presence is disliked...

... and if they go out, it is mustahabb for them to wear their casual clothes and not wear their best clothes, and it is mustahabb for them to wash themselves with water, and it is disliked for them to use perfume. All these rulings apply to old women who do not tempt desires and others like them. As for young or beautiful women, and those who tempt desires, it is disliked for them to be present at the prayer as their presence increases the danger of them causing fitna or being subject to it. If it is said: 'This is not in accordance with the hadeeth of Umm 'Atiyyah previously mentioned,' we reply, 'It has been reported in Saheeh Muslim and Bukhaari that 'A'isha, may Allaah be pleased with her said: "Had the Messenger of Allaah, may the peace and blessings of Allaah be upon him witnessed what the women have done of innovation, he would have forbidden them as the women of Bani Israa'eel were forbidden." And also because the types of fitna and causes of evil in these times are numerous, unlike the first age of the Muslims, and Allaah knows best.

I say: In our time, the situation is worse. Imaam Ibn Jawzee stated in his book *Kitaab Ahkaam an-Nisaa* [p. 38]:

I say that we have made clear that it is permissible for women to go out. However, if it is feared that there will be fitna on their part, or because of them, then it is better that they are prohibited from going out, because the men and women of the first generation of the Muslims were not like the men and women of this time.'

Meaning, the first generation of the Muslims were very religious. From these extracts, the Muslim sister should be aware that her attendance of the 'Eid prayer is

70

permitted Islamically on the condition that she adheres to the religious guidelines and principles of decency, and that by attending she has the intention of coming closer to Allaah, and joining the Muslims in their prayers and manifesting the rites of Islaam - and not to exhibit her beauty or expose herself to fitna.

Chapter 6

Laws Pertaining To Women Regarding Funerals

Allaah has written death on every soul while eternity is unique to him alone. Allaah says:

$$ ﴿ كُلُّ مَنْ عَلَيْهَا فَانٍ ۝ وَيَبْقَىٰ وَجْهُ رَبِّكَ ذُو الْجَلَالِ وَالْإِكْرَامِ ۝ ﴾ $$

"All that is on earth will perish; but will abide forever the Face of your Lord, Full of Majesty, Bounty and Honour." [Ar-Rahman: 26, 27]

He has decreed certain laws regarding the funerals of the sons of Adam whose execution is obligatory upon the living. Here, we shall mention the laws that relate specifically to women.

1. It is obligatory for women to undertake the washing of a dead woman's body, and it is not permissible for men to wash a woman's body except a husband; for him it is permissible to wash his wife's body. The opposite is also true (i.e. it is not permissible for women to wash the body of a man, but a wife can wash the body of her husband). This is because 'Ali, may Allah be pleased with him washed the body of his

72

wife Faatima, may Allah be pleased with her, the daughter of the Messenger of Allaah, may the peace and blessings of Allaah be upon him. Asmaa' Bint 'Umais, may Allaah be pleased with her washed her husband, Abu Bakr As-Siddeeq, may Allaah be pleased with him.

2. It is mustahabb to clothe the dead woman in five white sheets, including an Izaar (wrapper) around her waist, a Khimaar (covering) on her head, a chemise, and two sheets wrapped around her on top of these clothes. This is proved by what has been narrated by Layla Ath-Thaqafiyyah, may Allaah be pleased with her. She said: 'I was among those who washed Umm Kulthoom, may Allaah be pleased with her, the daughter of the Messenger of Allaah, may the peace and blessings of Allaah be upon him at the time of her death, and the first thing the Messenger of Allaah, may the peace and blessings of Allaah be upon him gave us was an Izaar (wrap), then a shirt, then a Khimaar, then a shroud. After that, she was placed in another sheet.' Narrated by Ahmad and Abu Dawud.

Imaam Shawkaani stated in *Nayl al-Awtaar* [4/42]:

This hadeeth indicates the permissibility of clothing the dead woman in a wrapper (Izaar), a shirt, a Khimaar, a shroud and a covering sheet placed over the body.

3. What must be done with the hair of a dead woman: It should be tied into three plaits, and placed behind her in accordance with the hadeeth of Umm 'Atiyyah, may Allaah be pleased with her which describes the washing

of the daughter of the Prophet, may the peace and blessings of Allaah be upon him, 'We plaited her hair into three plaits and placed them behind her.' Agreed upon.

4. The ruling concerning women following the funeral procession. It is narrated from Umm 'Atiyyah, may Allaah be pleased with her that she said: 'We were prohibited from following the funeral procession and it was not made firm upon us.' Agreed upon. The most apparent meaning of a statement of prohibition is that it is haraam. Regarding her statement '...and it was not made firm upon us':

Ibn Taymiyyah stated in *Majmu' al-Fataawa* [24/355]:

> It is possible that she meant that the prohibition was not emphasised, although this does not mean that the action is not haraam. Or it may be that she thought that the prohibition did not indicate that the action was haraam. However, sure proof is in the statement of the Prophet, may the peace and blessings of Allaah be upon him and not in the opinion of others.

5. The prohibition of women visiting the graves. It is narrated from Abu Hurairah, may Allah be pleased with him, that he said: 'The Messenger of Allaah, may the peace and blessings of Allaah be upon him cursed the women who visited the graves.' Narrated by Ahmad, Ibn Maajah and Tirmidhi and he authenticated it. Ibn Taymiyyah stated in *Majmu' al-Fataawa* [24/335-356]:

> It is clear that if this door is opened to the woman it makes her break down, lament and start to wail because

she is weak and easily prone to breaking down, and has little patience. Also, this action is a cause for the dead person to be punished, by her crying and the effect her voice and her appearance will have on the men. This has been stated in the hadeeth, 'For indeed, you make fitna for the living and you harm the dead.' Therefore, women visiting the graves can be a cause of actions that are haraam on their part, and on the part of men.

The extent to which their visiting could be a fitna cannot be clearly defined, as it is not possible to set a limit which one could say would not lead to fitna; and it is not possible to differentiate between one type of action or another. Among the fundamental principles of the Shari'ah is that the wisdom behind a ruling, if it is either hidden or not widespread, then the ruling is attached to the likely instance of the occurrence of that wisdom. So this action or this area is made haraam in order to prevent the occurrence of actions that are themselves haraam (even though this action in itself may be permissible). This is the same as the prohibition of seclusion with a woman (i.e. being alone with a woman in a room creates the possibility of illegal acts taking place)[5]. This action (i.e. her visiting the graves), does not contain any benefit except her supplication for the dead which she can, in any case, do in her house.

6. The prohibition of Niyaaha. Niyaaha means wailing in anguish, ripping ones clothes, pulling ones hair, and the slapping of cheeks and face in anguish, and

---

5 It is also the same as the prohibition of looking at the hidden beauty of a woman because of the fitna it leads to.

blackening and scratching ones face in agony, and uttering supplications of damnation and similar acts that show discontent with the divine decree of Allaah and His predestination, and lack of patience. All these acts are haraam and constitute one of the major sins as proved by the hadeeth in Bukhaari and Muslim in which the Messenger of Allaah, may the peace and blessings of Allaah be upon him said: 'Those who slap their cheeks in anguish, those who pull their hair out, and those who tear their clothes, and supplicate with the supplications of Jaahiliyyah are not of us.' Also in Bukhaari and Muslim it is mentioned that the Prophet, may the peace and blessings of Allaah be upon him distanced himself from the woman who screams when calamities occur; the woman who pulls her hair out; and the woman who tears her clothes. In *Saheeh Muslim* it is reported that the Prophet, may the peace and blessings of Allaah be upon him cursed the woman who committed Niyaaha, and the woman who listened to her – meaning a woman who seeks to hear the Niyaaha. So the Muslim Sister must ensure that she avoids these haraam actions at the time of calamity, and she must endure and have patience, so that the calamity will become expiation for her sins and an increase in her blessings. Allaah says:

$$ \text{﴿ وَلَنَبْلُوَنَّكُم بِشَىْءٍ مِّنَ ٱلْخَوْفِ وَٱلْجُوعِ وَنَقْصٍ مِّنَ ٱلْأَمْوَالِ وَٱلْأَنفُسِ وَٱلثَّمَرَٰتِ ۗ وَبَشِّرِ ٱلصَّٰبِرِينَ ۝ ٱلَّذِينَ إِذَآ أَصَٰبَتْهُم مُّصِيبَةٌ قَالُوٓاْ إِنَّا } $$

لِلَّهِ وَإِنَّا إِلَيْهِ رَاجِعُونَ ۝ أُوْلَٰٓئِكَ عَلَيْهِمْ صَلَوَٰتٌ مِّن رَّبِّهِمْ وَرَحْمَةٌ وَأُوْلَٰٓئِكَ هُمُ ٱلْمُهْتَدُونَ ۝

"Be sure We shall test you with something of fear, hunger, and loss of wealth, lives, and fruits (of your toil), but give glad tidings to those who patiently persevere – who when afflicted with calamity say: 'Truly! To Allah we belong and truly to Him is our return.' They are those on whom (descend) blessings from Allah and Mercy, and it is they who are the guided ones." [Al-Baqara: 155-157]

However, crying is permissible as long as it is not accompanied with wailing and other actions that are haraam actions, and does not show displeasure with Allaah's decree and His predestination. This is because in crying there is mercy for the dead, and it softens the heart, and is also unavoidable - thus it is permissible and may even be mustahabb. May Allaah help us.

Chapter 7

Laws Pertaining To Fasting

Fasting during the month of Ramadhaan is obligatory for every male and female Muslim. Fasting is one of the pillars of Islaam and one of its main foundations. Allaah says:

$$﴿ يَـٰٓأَيُّهَا ٱلَّذِينَ ءَامَنُوا۟ كُتِبَ عَلَيْكُمُ ٱلصِّيَامُ كَمَا كُتِبَ عَلَى ٱلَّذِينَ مِن قَبْلِكُمْ لَعَلَّكُمْ تَتَّقُونَ ١٨٣ ﴾$$

"O you who believe! Fasting is prescribed to you as it was prescribed to those before you, that you may attain *taqwa* (piety)." [Al-Baqara: 183]

So if a girl reaches adulthood, by witnessing one of the signs of puberty, including menstruation, then at that time the obligation of fasting applies to her. A girl may start to menstruate when she is nine years of age, and some of these girls may be ignorant that fasting is obligatory upon them at that time and they do not fast because they think they are still too young. Their families may not order them to fast, and this is a great mistake; leaving one of the pillars of Islaam. Any girl who does this must make up the fasting which she missed since the time she started to menstruate, even if a long period of time has passed, because she is still held

78

accountable for that fasting (and it is obligatory upon her, while making up her fasts, to feed a poor person half a saa' of food every day of the fasting).

Those on whom fasting is obligatory

If the month of Ramadhaan comes, it is obligatory upon every male and female adult Muslim in full health, and who is not travelling, to fast. Whoever is sick or travelling during the month, could break their fast and make up the number of days they missed at a later time. Allaah says:

$$ ﴿ فَمَن شَهِدَ مِنكُمُ ٱلشَّهْرَ فَلْيَصُمْهُ وَمَن كَانَ مَرِيضًا أَوْ عَلَىٰ سَفَرٍ فَعِدَّةٌ مِّنْ أَيَّامٍ أُخَرَ ﴾ $$

"So whoever is present (at his home, and not travelling) during that month should fast that month. But whoever is ill or on a journey, the same number of days (which one did not obeserve their fast must be made up) from other days." [Al-Baqara: 185]

In the same way, whoever witnesses the month but is of old age and is not capable of fasting, or has a sickness which is permanent, without any hope of its being cured at any time in the future, whether male or female, should break their fast and feed a poor person every day, half a saa' of the staple food of the locality. Allaah says:

$$\{ وَعَلَى الَّذِينَ يُطِيقُونَهُ فِدْيَةٌ طَعَامُ مِسْكِينٍ \}$$

"And as for those who can fast with difficulty is a ransom: the feeding of one poor person (for every day)." [Al-Baqara: 184]

Abdullah Ibn 'Abbaas, may Allaah be pleased with him said: 'This is for the old person who has no hope of recovery.' Narrated by Bukhaari. The same ruling applies for a sick person who has an incurable sickness - they do not have to make up the fast because of their incapability.

A woman has certain specific excuses that make it permissible for her to break her fast during the month of Ramadhaan, on the condition that she makes up the days that she misses because of these excuses.

1. Menstruation and post-birth bleeding. It is not permissible for a woman to fast while in these two states, and it is obligatory upon her to make up the days later. This is proved by what is reported in Saheeh Bukhaari and Muslim from 'A'isha, may Allaah be pleased with her who said: 'We were ordered to make up the fasting and we were not ordered to make up the prayer.' She said this when she a woman asked her: 'Why is it that the menstruating woman makes up the fasts but does not make up the prayers?' She explained that this is one of the matters that are based absolutely on revelation, and we simply follow what has been decreed in the Qur'an and Sunnah.

As for the wisdom behind this, Ibn Taymiyyah stated in *Majmu' al-Fataawa* [25/251]

> A woman loses her blood through the menstrual blood that leaves her body. The menstruating woman is capable of fasting at times other than during her menstruation, during which her own blood leaves her body. Fasting in this condition is easy, as no blood that strengthens the body is being lost. Fasting during her menstruation would mean that blood that nourishes her body and is part of it would be lost, and this would entail the weakening of her body, and fasting would become difficult, and thus she has been ordered to fast outside of her menstruation.

2. Pregnancy and Breast-feeding: if fasting while a woman is pregnant or is breast-feeding will harm her or her child or both of them, then she should break her fast. If the harm that caused her to break her fast affected only her child, and not herself, then she must make up the days she missed and feed a poor person against each day she missed. If the harm were to affect her only, then she would only make up the fasts she missed. This is because both the pregnant woman and the breastfeeding woman are included in the statement of Allaah:

$$ \text{﴿ وَعَلَى ٱلَّذِينَ يُطِيقُونَهُۥ فِدْيَةٌ طَعَامُ مِسْكِينٍ ﴾} $$

"And as for those who can fast with difficulty is a ransom: the feeding of one poor person (for every day)." [Al-Baqara: 184]

Al Haafidh Ibn Katheer said in his Tafseer [1/739]:

Included in this meaning is the pregnant woman and the woman who is breastfeeding if they fear for themselves or their children.

Ibn Taymiyyah said in *Majmu' al-Fataawa* [25/318]:

If the pregnant woman fears for her foetus, then she should break her fast and make up every day and feed a poor person one-unit weight of bread against each of the days she missed.

Notes

1. The woman afflicted with false menstruation (see previous chapter). This is the woman who sees blood that is not due to menstruation as has previously been mentioned. It is obligatory for her to fast, and it is not permissible for her to break her fast as a result of this type of blood. Ibn Taymiyyah, after mentioning the breaking of the fast in the case of the menstruating woman, said [25/251]:

...Unlike false menstruation, because it could occur at any time, and thus the woman may not have a chance to make up the fasts she misses. This is unavoidable, like vomiting, bleeding from a wound, pus, or nocturnal emissions and similar things which can occur at any time, making it impossible to predict, so they are not considered as anything that negate fasting, like the blood of menstruation.

2. It is obligatory for the menstruating woman, the pregnant woman, and the woman who is breastfeeding to make up the days that they have missed (during Ramadhaan) at the end of the month of Ramadhaan

before the next Ramadhaan. It is better for them to make up the fasts early and if there only remains between the beginning of the next Ramadhaan the number of days that she missed then it becomes obligatory upon her to fast those days so that she doesn't enter the next Ramadhaan while she still has fasts from the last Ramadhaan to make up. If she does not do this, and she enters the next Ramadhaan and she did not have an excuse in delaying those fasts, she still has to make them up and she also has to feed a poor person against each day. If she did have an excuse, she only has to make up the missing days. The same conditions or rulings apply to the woman who broke her fast due to sickness or travelling.

3. It is not permissible for a woman to fast a non-obligatory fast if her husband is with her unless she has his permission. This is proved by what is narrated from Bukhaari and Muslim and others from Abu Hurairah, may Allah be pleased with him that the Prophet, may the peace and blessings of Allaah be upon him said: 'It is not permissible for a woman to fast while her husband is present unless with his permission.' In some narrations of Ahmad and Abu Dawud,'... except for the fasting of the month of Ramadhaan.' However, if her husband grants her permission to fast a non-obligatory fast, or her husband is not with her, or she is unmarried, then it is mustahabb for her to fast, particularly on the days which are mustahabb to fast, like Mondays and Thursdays, the three days of every lunar month, the six days in the month of Shawwal, and the ten days of Dhul-Hijjah, and

the days of 'Arafah and 'Ashurah along with the day before and after it. However, it is not appropriate for her to fast a non-obligatory fast while she still has to make up days she missed from Ramadhaan, until she has made those days up, and Allaah knows best.

4. If the menstruating woman regains her state of purity during the daytime in the month of Ramadhaan, she should abstain from eating and drinking for the remainder of the day, and make up the entire day along with the days that she missed due to her menstruation. Her abstinence for the remainder of the day on which she regained her purity is obligatory for her out of reverence for the period (of Ramadhaan).

Chapter 8

Laws Pertaining To Hajj & 'Umra

The Hajj pilgrimage to the Sacred House of Allaah, every year is a general obligation on the Muslims. Any Muslim who satisfies the conditions that make Hajj compulsory must perform the Hajj at least once in a lifetime - to perform Hajj more than once is an optional form of worship. Hajj is one of the Pillars of Islaam. It also represents the woman's Jihaad as is stated in the hadeeth of A'isha, may Allaah be pleased with her when she said: 'O Messenger of Allaah, is Jihaad compulsory on women?' He replied, 'Yes, a Jihaad which involves no fighting - the Hajj and the 'Umra.' Narrated by Ahmad and Ibn Maajah with an authentic chain. Imaam Bukhaari narrates that she, may Allaah be pleased with her said: 'O Messenger of Allaah, we consider Jihaad as being the best of actions - should we (women) not perform Jihaad ?' He said: 'But (indeed) the best Jihaad is the accepted Hajj.'

Rulings specific to women on Hajj

1. The Mahram (a male relation of the woman to whom she is not allowed to be married). Hajj has several general conditions that apply to both men and women:

the person must be a Muslim, sane, free (i.e. not a slave), adult (past puberty), and financially capable. The woman has an extra condition to meet: She must be accompanied by a mahram who travels with her - this is her husband, or one to whom she is prohibited permanently from marrying because of kinship, like her father, her son, her brother; or because of another specified reason, like he being her foster-relation, or her step-father or step-son. The proof for this is what Ibn 'Abbaas, may Allaah be pleased with him narrated that he heard the Prophet, may the peace and blessings of Allaah be upon him giving a Khutba, (religious speech) in which he said: 'It is not permissible for a man to be left secluded alone with a woman unless she is accompanied by a mahram. And a woman is not permitted to travel unless she is accompanied by a mahram.' A man rose up and said: 'O Messenger of Allaah, my wife has left to perform Hajj and I have been registered in the military expedition of so-and-so.' He said: 'Then leave and perform the Hajj with your wife.' Agreed upon. Ibn 'Umar, may Allaah be pleased with him said: 'The Messenger of Allaah, may the peace and blessings of Allaah be upon him said: "It is not permissible for a woman to travel three days unless she is accompanied by a mahram."' Agreed upon. There are many other hadeeths that prohibit a woman from travelling for Hajj and other purposes without a Mahram. This is because a woman is weak and subject to obstacles, and things that may harm her during her travel, which only a man could handle. Secondly, a woman is a temptation for evildoers, so it is absolutely necessary to have a mahram who will protecte her from their evil. The Mahram who will accompany her for the Hajj must himself also fulfil the following conditions: he must be Muslim, sane, and adult. She would not be safe with a disbeliever. If she is unable to find a mahram she must deputise another person to perform the Hajj on her behalf.

2. If the Hajj is not obligatory for her, and she wishes to perform it, she must first seek the permission of her husband - as by performing Hajj she is depriving him of his marital right. In *al-Mughni* [3/240]:

> As for the non-obligatory Hajj, then it is permissible for the husband to disallow her. Ibn al-Mundhir said: 'There is a consensus among the scholars from whom knowledge is taken that the husband can disallow his wife from leaving to perform a non-obligatory Hajj. The reason for this is that the right of the husband is an obligation upon her, and so she is not permitted to abandon this right for something which is not obligatory.

3. It is permissible for a woman to perform the Hajj and 'Umra on behalf of a man. Ibn Taymiyyah stated in *Majmu' al-Fataawa*:

> The scholars are agreed that it is permissible for a woman to perform the Hajj on behalf of another woman, whether she is her daughter or not; and it is also permissible for a woman to perform Hajj on behalf of a man, according to the majority of the scholars including the Four Imaams. This is as ordered by the Prophet, may the peace and blessings of Allaah be upon him when he ordered the woman from the Khath'am tribe to

perform the Hajj on behalf of her father, when she said: 'O Messenger of Allaah, the obligation of Allaah upon his servants to perform Hajj has fallen on my father in his old age,' so he ordered her to perform the Hajj for her father, even though the state of Ihraam for a man is more complete than that of a woman (i.e. the Ihraam for a man involves more restrictions than that of a woman, and is thus more rewarding).

4. If while the woman is travelling for the Hajj she starts menstruating or after-birth bleeding, she should continue her travel as the other women do, as it is not a condition for the state of Ihraam to be in a state of ritual purity. In *al-Mughni* [3/293-294]:

...Taking a bath is instructed for women at the time of getting into Ihraam, in the same way that it is instructed for men, as it is one of the rituals of the pilgrimage. It is stronger in the case of the menstruating woman and the woman bleeding from childbirth; as there are narrations that specifically mention their cases. Jaabir said: 'When we came to Dhul-Hulaifah and Asmaa' Bint Umais gave birth to Muhammad Ibn Abu Bakr, she sent a message to the Messenger of Allaah, may the peace and blessings of Allaah be upon him asking what she should do. He said: 'Take a bath and use a pad, and assume the state of Ihraam.'' Narrated by Muslim. From Ibn 'Abbaas, the Prophet, may the peace and blessings of Allaah be upon him said: 'The women who are bleeding after childbirth and the menstruating women, if blood comes to them at the time, they should assume Ihraam and perform all the rituals of pilgrimage except for Tawaaf of the House.' Narrated by Abu Dawud. The Prophet, may the peace and blessings of Allaah be upon him ordered A'isha, may Allaah be pleased with her to take a bath at the time of making the intention for the Hajj while she was menstruating.

The wisdom behind the taking of a ritual bath by the menstruating woman and the woman who has just given birth when going into the state of Ihraam, is for hygiene and removal of offensive smells, in order that she does not offend other people when they congregate, and also to lessen the impurity. If the menstruation or post-birth bleeding occurs while she is in the state of Ihraam, they do not affect her Ihraam; she remains in Ihraam and stays away from the prohibitions of Ihraam. These women do not perform Tawaaf of the Ka'ba until they become pure from the menstruation or post-birth bleeding and take their baths. If the day of 'Arafaat arrives and they have not regained their purity, and they had assumed Ihraam for 'Umra (intending to renew the Ihraam for Hajj), then they should assume the Ihraam for Hajj and join it to the 'Umra so that it becomes like a combined (Qiraan) Hajj. The proof of this is that A'isha, may Allaah be pleased with her menstruated after she had assumed Ihraam for 'Umra. The Prophet, may the peace and blessings of Allaah be upon him came to her while she was crying. He said: 'Why are you crying? May be you are menstruating?' she replied, 'Yes.' He said: 'This is something that Allaah has ordained for the daughters of Adam. (Continue and) do everything the Hajj pilgrim does, except do not perform Tawaaf of the House.' Narrated by Bukhaari and Muslim.

In the hadeeth of Jaabir, which is agreed upon: 'The Messenger of Allaah, may the peace and blessings of Allaah be upon him came to A'isha, may Allaah be pleased with her and found her weeping, and said: "What is the matter with you?" She said: "I have entered in the monthly period, and the people have left the state of Ihraam, but I did not and I have not done Tawaaf of the House. The people are going for Hajj now (but I cannot go)," Whereupon he said: "This is something which Allaah has ordained for the daughters of Adam, so take a bath, and put on Ihraam for Hajj." She (A'isha, may Allaah be pleased with her) did accordingly, and was present at all the places of congregation till the monthly period was over. She then circled the House, and (walked between) Safaa and Marwa. He (the Prophet, may the peace and blessings of Allaah be upon him) then said: "Now both your Hajj and Umra are complete."'

Ibn Qayyim said in *Tahtheeb As-Sunnah* [2/303]:

The sahih hadeeths are clear in that she had assumed Ihraam for 'Umra firstly, and then the Messenger of Allaah, may the peace and blessings of Allaah be upon him ordered her when she menstruated to assume Ihraam for Hajj so she became a Qaarin (one who combines the two rituals of Hajj and Umra at the same time) and because of this the Prophet, may the peace and blessings of Allaah be upon him said to her, 'Your tawaaf of the house and between Safaa and Marwa suffices you for your Hajj and 'Umra.'

5. What the woman should do at the time of assuming Ihraam. She does just as a man does in terms of washing and cleaning and cutting the nails and hair as is necessary and removing offensive odours, so that she will not need to do that during Ihraam when she will be prevented from doing so. If she does not need to do any of these things, then she does not have to do them and they are not part of the specific duties of Ihraam. There is no harm for her to perfume her body with perfume that does not have a sharp fragrance. This is proved by the hadeeth of 'A'isha, may Allaah be pleased with her: 'We used to go with the Messenger of Allaah, may the peace and blessings of Allaah be upon him, and we would apply musk to our foreheads at the time of Ihraam. If we perspired, the perfume would run down onto our faces, and the Prophet, may the peace and blessings of Allaah be upon him would see it, and not prohibit us.' Narrated by Abu Dawud. Shawkaani stated in *Nayl al-Awtaar* [5/12]:

His silence indicates permissibility because he does not remain silent about things which are wrong.

6. At the time of making the *Niyyah* (intention) for Ihraam, the woman takes off her Burqa and her Niqaab if she happens to be wearing them before the Ihraam. They are both veils that cover the face, which have two holes for the eyes through which the woman can see. This is proved by the statement of the Prophet, may the peace and blessings of Allaah be upon him: 'The female muhrim should not wear the Niqaab.' Narrated by Bukhaari. The Burqa is stronger than the Niqaab (and

therefore this hadeeth applies to it). She takes off whatever she has on her hands like her gloves if she was wearing them before the Ihraam. She should cover her face with something other than the Niqaab or Burqa by placing her head cover or a cloth when she is in sight of men who are not her mahrams. Also, she should cover her hands without using gloves by wrapping them with some form of cloth because the face and the hands are among the parts of her body that must be hidden from men during Ihraam and outside Ihraam. Ibn Taymiyyah said:

> And as for the woman, she is (entirely) 'awrah, and because of this, it is permissible for her to wear clothes which cover her, and she is allowed to seek shade under her camel-borne litter. However, the Prophet, may the peace and blessings of Allaah be upon him prohibited her to wear Niqaab or gloves... The gloves are a covering made specially for the hand, but it is permissible by the agreement of the scholars for her to cover her face with anything that does not come into contact with her face. If it comes into contact with her face, the correct ruling is that this it is also permissible. The woman is not obligated to distance the covering from her face with her hand, a piece of wood, or anything else, because the Prophet, may the peace and blessings of Allaah be upon him made no distinction between her face and her hands. Both are treated like the body of a man, and not like his head. The Prophet's wives, may the peace and blessings of Allaah be upon him used to let the cloth fall on their faces without regard for making a gap between the cover and their faces. It has not been reported from any of the scholars

that the Prophet, may the peace and blessings of Allaah be upon him said that the Ihraam of a woman is with regard to her face and in fact this is the statement of some of the Salaf (Pious Predecessors).

Ibn Qayyim stated in *Tahtheeb As-Sunan* [2/350]:

Not a single statement has been reported from the Prophet, may the peace and blessings of Allaah be upon him regarding the obligation of the woman uncovering her face at the time of her Ihraam except for the prohibition of wearing the Niqaab...

... It was narrated from Asmaa', may Allaah be pleased with her, that she used to cover her face while she was in the state of Ihraam. A'isha, may Allaah be pleased with her said: 'Riders used to approach us when we were in the company of the Messenger of Allaah, may the peace and blessings of Allaah be upon him while we were in the state of Ihraam. If they came close to us, we would lower the Jilbaab from our heads onto our faces. When they passed us, we would uncover (our faces).' Abu Dawud mentioned this.

So the Muslim sister in the state of Ihraam should be aware that it is not permissible to cover her face and hands with things tailored to fit their shapes, in particular the Niqaab and gloves. She should also know that it is obligatory for her to conceal her face and hands from men who are not her mahrams with a Khimaar, cloth or similar things, and that there is no proof to place anything which raises the cover from the face like a piece of wood or a turban, or anything else.

7. It is permissible for the woman to wear any women's clothes she pleases which are not attractive or resemble the clothes of men, or are tight-fitting - showing the dimensions of her limbs, or transparent - not concealing what is underneath, or too short - not covering her legs or hands, but instead should be abundant, thick, and wide. Ibn al-Mundhir said: as quoted in *al-Mughni* [3/328]:

> There is a consensus among the scholars that the woman in Ihraam can wear shirts, vests, baggy trousers, khimaars, and leather socks.

She does not have to wear a particular colour (such as green) and can instead wear any colours she desires from among those specific to women (such as dark red, green, or black). It is also permissible for her to change these colours if she wishes.

8. It is Sunnah for her to pronounce the *Talbiyyah* after she has assumed Ihraam loud enough for her to hear herself. Ibn Abd al-Barr said as quoted in *al-Mughni* [3/330-331]:

> There is a consensus amongst the scholars that it is Sunnah for the woman not to raise her voice. Instead, she should only pronounce it loud enough to hear herself. It is disliked for her to raise her voice because of the fitna she may cause, and for this reason it is not Sunnah for her to pronounce the Adhaan or the Iqaama, and the Sunnah for her in order to alert the Imaam while in prayer is for her to clap her hands, and not to raise her voice to make the glorification of Allaah (as it is for men).

9. It is obligatory upon her to cover herself fully in Tawaaf, to lower her voice, to lower her gaze and not to jostle with men, particularly at the Black Stone and at the Yemeni corner. It is better for her to perform her tawaaf at the farthest point away from the House, without bumping with men, than making tawaaf near to the Ka'ba and thus bumping with men. This is because crowding with men is haraam because of the fitna it entails. As for coming near to the Ka'ba and kissing the stone, these acts are Sunnah for her if they are easy for her to accomplish. A haraam act should not be committed in order to fulfil a Sunnah act. Instead in this situation, the act does not become Sunnah for her. This is because the Sunnah, as it applies to her in this situation, is to point to the Black Stone if she passes it. Imaam Nawawi stated in *al-Majmu'* [8/37]:

> Our companions say, 'It is not mustahabb for the woman to kiss the stone or to touch it unless the area of Tawaaf is empty at night, or other times, because of the harm the women cause and can be affected by.

In *al-Mughni* [3/331]:

> And it is mustahabb for the woman to make tawaaf at night because it conceals her better, and there is less crowding, and also at that time it is possible for her to come close to the House and touch the stone.

10. In *al-Mughni* [3/394]:

> And the tawaaf of the women and their sa'i are both (completed) at a walking pace. Ibn al-Mundhir says, 'There is a consensus among the scholars that there is no ramal (jogging) for the women neither around the

house, nor between Safaa and Marwa and they do not have to uncover their right shoulders during tawaaf as men do. This is because the reason for these two acts is to make a show of strength, and this is not intended in the case of women. Instead concealment is what is desired from her; and if she were to jog and uncover her shoulders she would be exhibiting herself.

11. What the menstruating woman must and must not do among the acts of Hajj until she regains purity. The menstruating woman should perform all the rights of the Hajj, including Ihraam, standing at 'Arafaat, staying the night at Muzdalifah and stoning the Jamaraat. She should not perform tawaaf of the House until she regains purity, because of the statement of the Prophet, may the peace and blessings of Allaah be upon him to 'A'isha, may Allaah be pleased with her, at the time of her menstruation: 'Do everything that the Pilgrim does, but do not make tawaaf of the House until you regain purity.' Agreed upon. In another narration by Muslim: 'Do as the Pilgrim does, but do not perform tawaaf of the House until you take your bath.'

Al-Shawkaani stated in *Nayl al-Awtaar* [5/49]:

This hadeeth is clear in prohibiting the menstruating woman from making tawaaf until the blood stops and she has washed herself. A statement of prohibition necessitates nullification, and thus the tawaaf of the menstruating woman is invalid. This is the position of the majority of the scholars. She does not do the Sa'i between Safaa and Marwa, because Sa'i is not valid unless it occurs after a tawaaf, because the Prophet, may the peace and blessings of Allaah be upon him never did the Sa'i except after a tawaaf.

Imaam Nawawi stated in *al-Majmu'* [8/82]:

Section: If a person performed Sa'i before tawaaf, his Sa'i is not correct in our opinion, and this is the position of the majority of scholars. Previously, we have mentioned that al-Maawardi related the consensus of the scholars on this point, and it is the madhhab of Maalik, Abu Haneefa, and Ahmad. Ibn al-Mundhir quoted 'Ataa and some of (the scholars of) Ahl-Hadeeth (stating) that it is correct. Our companions relate this to 'Ataa and Dawud.

Our proof is that the Prophet, may the peace and blessings of Allaah be upon him performed Sa'i only after tawaaf, and he said: 'You must take your rites of pilgrimage from me.' As for the hadeeth of Ibn Shuraik the sahaabi, (in which) he said 'I went with the Messenger of Allaah, may the peace and blessings of Allaah be upon him for the Hajj, and people were coming to him (to ask him questions), some saying "O Messenger of Allaah, I performed Sa'i before Tawaaf," or "I delayed such-and-such," or "I did such-and-such before another," and he would reply, "There is no harm in these acts; the only harm is on the man who unjustly defames the honour of a Muslim, such a one is the one who has perished and caused harm."' Narrated by Abu Dawud with an authentic chain. All of its narrators are narrators included in Bukhaari and Muslim except 'Usamah Ibn Shuraik, the sahaabi. The interpretation of this hadeeth is what al-Khattaabi and others said: that this statement 'I performed Sa'i before Tawaaf,' means 'I performed Sa'i after Tawaaf al-Qudoom and before Tawaaf al-Ifaadaa.'

Our Shaykh Muhammad al-Ameen Ash-Shanqeeti stated in his Tafseer *Adhwaa al-Bayaan* [5/252]:

Know that the majority of the scholars are of the opinion that Sa'i is not acceptable except after tawaaf. So if a person were to perform Sa'i before tawaaf, it would not be acceptable in the view of the majority of the scholars, including the four Imaams. Al-Maawardi and others have reported the consensus of the scholars on this point.

Then he quoted the words of Nawawi previously mentioned, and his answer to the hadeeth of Ibn Shuraik. Then he said:

His statement, 'before I made tawaaf', means the Tawaaf of Ifaadaa which is a pillar of the rites of Hajj and this does not negate that he made Sa'i after Tawaaf al-Qudoom, which is not a pillar of the rites of Hajj.

In *al-Mughni* [5/240, Hijr Edition]:

The Sa'i follows tawaaf and is not correct unless tawaaf comes before it. Sa'i before it is not acceptable, and this is the position of Maalik, Shaafi'i and the scholars who accept Qiyaas as proof. Ataa says, 'It is permissible.' From Ahmad, 'It is permissible if the person forgot. If the person did it on purpose, his Sa'i is not permissible because the Prophet, may the peace and blessings of Allaah be upon him, when he was asked about Sa'i preceding the tawaaf if the person was ignorant or forgetful, replied "There is no harm."' The point behind the first position is that the Prophet, may the peace and blessings of Allaah be upon him actually performed Sa'i after his tawaaf and said: 'You must take your rites of pilgrimage from me.'

So it is clear from what has preceded that the hadeeth which is used by those who say that the Sa'i before the tawaaf is acceptable, is not a proof for this, because it has one of two interpretations: it either concerns someone who performed the Sa'i before Tawaaf al-Ifaadha while he had already performed Sa'i for Tawaaf al-Qudoom, so his Sa'i actually occured after a tawaaf, or it refers to the ignorant or forgetful person, and does not include the person who does it on purpose. I have dwelt long on this point because there are those who issue fatwaas now saying it is permissible to perform the Sa'i before tawaaf in any situation, and may Allaah help us.

Note

1. If a woman performed tawaaf and before finishing she started menstruating, in this situation she should perform the Sa'i, because purity is not a condition for Sa'i. In *al-Mughni* [5/246]:

> Most of the scholars are of the opinion that purity is not a condition for the validity of Sa'i between Safaa and Marwa. Among those who said this are 'Ataa, Maalik, Shafi'i, Abu Thawr, and the People of Ra'iy (those who accept Qiyaas as a proof)...

> ...Abu Dawud said: 'I heard Ahmad say, "If a woman performs tawaaf of the house then menstruates, she does Sa'i between Safaa and Marwa and then leaves. It has

been narrated from 'A'isha, may Allaah be pleased with her and Umm Salama, may Allaah be pleased with her that they said: 'If a woman performs tawaaf of the house and then prays the two rakaats of tawaaf, then menstruates, she should perform Sa'i between Safaa and Marwa. Narrated by al-Athram.'"

2. It is permissible for the women to leave along with the weak or sick people from Muzdalifah after the setting of the moon, and to stone Jamarat al-Akabah after arriving at Mina for fear of the crowds.

Al-Muwaffaq stated in *al-Mughni* [5/286]:

There is no harm for the weak and the women to leave early. Among those who used to let the weak of his family leave early was Abd ar-Rahman ibn Awf and 'A'isha, may Allaah be pleased with them. This was the position of 'Ataa, ath-Thawri, Shafi'i, Abu Thawr and the People of Ra'iy, and we do not know of any disagreement regarding this point. Another reason is because it makes it easy for them and it dispels from them the difficulties of crowding, and it is in accordance with the action of their Prophet, may the peace and blessings of Allaah be upon him.

Imaam Shawkani stated in *Nayl al-Awtar* [5/70]:

The proofs indicate that the time for stoning for those who do not have an excuse is after the rising of the sun. Whoever does have an excuse, however, such as women and others like the weak, are allowed (to do the stoning) before that.

Imaam Nawawi stated in *al-Majmu'* [8/125]:

Shafi'i and the companions say, 'The sunnah is to let the weak, from among the women and others, leave early from Muzdalifah before dawn after half of the night, to go to Mina and stone Jamarat al-Aqabah before the crowding of the people...

Then he mentioned the hadeeths that indicate this.

3. For Hajj and 'Umra, the woman should cut her hair from the end of her locks by about the length of an *unmulah*. It is not permissible for her to shave her scalp. An *unmulah* is the last joint of the finger to its tip. In *al-Mughni* [5/310, Hijr Edition]:

It is decreed for the woman to shorten (her hair) without shaving and there is no disagreement (between the scholars) regarding this. Ibn al-Mundhir said: 'There is a consensus of the People of Knowledge on this, and this is because shaving in their case is mutilation.' Ibn 'Abbaas, may Allaah be pleased with him said: 'The Messenger of Allaah, may the peace and blessings of Allaah be upon him said: "Women should not shave their hair. Instead, they should shorten it."' Narrated by Abu Dawud. From 'Ali, may Allah be pleased with him, he said: 'The Messenger of Allaah, may the peace and blessings of Allaah be upon him prohibited the woman from shaving her head.' Narrated by At-Tirmidhi. Ahmad used to say, 'The length of a fingertip should be cut from every plait,' and this is the statement of Ibn 'Umar, Shafi'i, Ishaaq and Abu Thawr. Abu Dawud said: 'I heard Ahmad (when he was) asked about a woman who shortened (the hair) from all parts of her head. He said: "Yes, she gathers her hair to the front of her head, and then cuts from the ends of her hair the length of a fingertip."'

Imaam Naawi stated in *al-Majmu'* [8/150, 154]:

> The scholars have a concensus that the woman is ordered not to shave her head, instead she should shorten her hair because shaving in their case is an innovation and a mutilation.

4. If the menstruating woman has stoned the Jamarat al-Aqabah, and shortened her hair, then she is free from the restrictions of the state of Ihraam, and the things which were prohibited for her become permissible again - except that she cannot have sexual intercourse with her husband, so she should not give him access to her, until she has performed Tawaaf al-Ifaadah around the House. If he were to have intercourse with her during this period, she must pay the Fidya (penalty). This is to sacrifice one animal from the sheep genus in Makkah, and distribute its meat among the poor people of Makkah. This is the judgement because the intercourse took place after the first disengagement from the state of Ihraam.

5. If the woman were to menstruate after Tawaaf al-Ifaadah, she could then travel whenever she pleased, and the obligation of Tawaaf al-Wadaa' (the Farewell Tawaaf) does not apply to her. This is proven by the hadeeth of 'A'isha, may Allaah be pleased with her, when she said: 'Safiah Bint Huyaiy menstruated after she had performed Tawaaf al-Ifaadah. She said: "So I informed the Messenger of Allaah, may the peace and blessings of Allaah be upon him." He said: "Is she going to delay us?" I said: "O Messenger of Allaah, she has already performed Tawaaf al-Ifaadah around the House,

and she menstruated after this." He said: "Then she can leave." Agreed upon.

Narrated from Ibn Abbaas, may Allaah be pleased with him: 'The people were ordered to make the Tawaaf of the House, as their last contact with the House, except menstruating women for whom permission has been given.' Ageed upon. Also narrated from him is that the Prophet, may the peace and blessings of Allaah be upon him, 'Made an allowance for the menstruating woman to leave before she had performed Tawaaf (al-Wadaa), if she had already performed Tawaaf al-Ifaadah.' Narrated by Ahmad. Imaam Nawawi stated in *al-Majmu'* [8/218]:

Ibn al-Mundhir stated, 'This is the position of most of the scholars, including Maalik, al-Awzaa'i, ath-Thawri, Ishaaq, Abu Thawr, Abu Haneefa and others.'

In *al-Mughni*[3/461]:

This is the position of the majority of the Scholars of the regions…

…The ruling for the woman who has post-birth bleeding is the same as for the menstruating woman, as the laws of nifaas are the same as the laws of menstruation as regards the obligation or non-obligation of religious duties.

6. It is mustahab for the woman to visit the Prophet's Masjid, may the peace and blessings of Allaah be upon him, in order to pray there and supplicate, although it is not permissible for her to visit the Prophet's grave, may the peace and blessings of Allaah be upon him, as she has been prohibited from visiting the graves. Shaykh

Muhammad Ibn Ibraheem Aal Shaykh, the Mufti of Saudi Arabia stated in his collection of Fatwas [3/239]:

> The correct position regarding this issue is that women are prohibited from visiting the Prophet's grave, may the peace and blessings of Allaah be upon him, for two reasons:
>
> i) The generality of the proofs. If a prohibition is stated generally, then it is not permissible for anyone to exclude something from this general applicability, unless he has a proof.
>
> ii) The reason behind this ruling is also found in this case (i.e. the reason why women are not allowed to visit the graves also applies to the Prophet's grave, may the peace and blessings of Allaah be upon him).

Shaykh Abdul Azeez Ibn Baaz, may Allaah have mercy on him stated in his guide to the pilgrimage, when writing about visiting the grave of the Messenger of Allaah, may the peace and blessings of Allaah be upon him for the person who visits his Holy Masjid:

> This visit has been ordained for men only. As for the women, they are not permitted to visit the graves, as it has been established from the Prophet, may the peace and blessings of Allaah be upon him that he cursed the women who visited the graves, and those who build shrines and Masjids over the graves.
>
> As for intending to go to Madeena in order to pray in the Masjid of the Messenger, to supplicate, and other things that are permitted in all Masjids, that is permissible for both men and women.

Chapter 9

Laws Pertaining To Marriage & Divorce

Allaah says:

﴿ وَمِنْ ءَايَٰتِهِۦٓ أَنْ خَلَقَ لَكُم مِّنْ أَنفُسِكُمْ أَزْوَٰجًا لِّتَسْكُنُوٓا۟ إِلَيْهَا وَجَعَلَ بَيْنَكُم مَّوَدَّةً وَرَحْمَةً إِنَّ فِي ذَٰلِكَ لَـَٔايَٰتٍ لِّقَوْمٍ يَتَفَكَّرُونَ ﴿٢١﴾ ﴾

"And among His Signs is that He created for you mates from among yourselves, that you may find repose in them, and He has put between you love and mercy. Verily in that indeed are signs for those who reflect." [Ar-Rum: 21]

Allaah says:

﴿ وَأَنكِحُوا۟ ٱلْأَيَٰمَىٰ مِنكُمْ وَٱلصَّٰلِحِينَ مِنْ عِبَادِكُمْ وَإِمَآئِكُمْ إِن يَكُونُوا۟ فُقَرَآءَ يُغْنِهِمُ ٱللَّهُ مِن فَضْلِهِۦ وَٱللَّهُ وَٰسِعٌ عَلِيمٌ ﴿٣٢﴾ ﴾

"And get those among you who are single married, and the virtuous ones among your slaves, male or female. If they are in poverty Allaah will enrich them out of His Bounty. And Allaah is All-Sufficient (for the needs of His creatures), and knows all things." [An-Nur: 32]

Imaam Ibn Katheer commenting on this verse said: 'This is an order to marry. Some of the scholars have taken this order to be obligatory upon any person who is able to do so. They have also used as proof the Prophet's statement, may the peace and blessings of Allaah be upon him: 'O company of young people, whoever is (financially) capable of marriage, should get married because this protects the gaze and the chastity of the private parts. Whoever is not able to marry, then he should fast because it is a shield for him.' Narrated by Bukhaari and Muslim from the hadeeth of Ibn Mas'ood, may Allaah be pleased with him. Then he mentioned that marriage is one of the causes of attaining wealth using as a proof Allaah's statement:

$$﴿ إِن يَكُونُوا۟ فُقَرَآءَ يُغْنِهِمُ ٱللَّهُ مِن فَضْلِهِۦٓ ﴾$$

"If they are in poverty Allaah will enrich them out of His Bounty." [An-Nur: 32]

He mentioned that Abu Bakr As-Siddeeq, may Allaah be pleased with him said: 'Obey Allaah in what he has ordered you concerning marriage, and He will fulfil His promise of wealth to you.'

From Ibn Masood, may Allaah be pleased with him: 'Seek wealth through marriage. Allaah says:

$$\text{﴿ إِن يَكُونُوا۟ فُقَرَآءَ يُغْنِهِمُ ٱللَّهُ مِن فَضْلِهِۦ ﴾}$$

"If they are in poverty Allaah will enrich them out of His Bounty." [An-Nur: 32]

Ibn Jareer narrated it, and al-Baghawi narrated a similar statement from 'Umar, may Allaah be pleased with him. [5/94-95, Dar al-Andaloos Edition].

Ibn Taymiyyah stated in *Majmu al-Fataawa* [32-90]:

Allaah has made permissible for the believers to marry and to divorce, and to marry the divorced woman after she has married someone else. And the Christians have made it haraam for some of them to marry (monks, nuns). Those to whom marriage is permissible, they have made divorce haraam. The Jews allow divorce, but if the divorced woman marries another man, she can never remarry her first husband. The Christians do not have divorce, and the Jews do not allow remarriage after marrying someone else. Allaah has made both actions permissible for the believers.

Imaam Ibn al-Qayyim stated in the book *al-Hady an-Nabawi* [3/149]: explaining the benefits of sex, which is one of the objectives of marriage:

The reason for sex is to attain three basic objectives. The first is protection of lineage and the continuation of genus until the end of the time that Allaah has destined for this world. The second is the release of semen, which is harmful if it remains in the body. The third is the fulfilment of desire and enjoyment of blessing.

So marriage has great benefits, the greatest of which is that it is a protection from fornication, and it helps in lowering the gaze from things that are haraam; it is also the means of continuation of the progeny of mankind and the protection of lineage. The benefits also include the attainment of harmony between the married couples, and psychological stability, as well as the mutual co-operation between them in the creation of a righteous family - which is one of the building blocks of a Muslim society. Among the benefits also is the responsibility the husband takes to support the woman and take care of her, and the responsibility the woman undertakes to do the housework and the fulfilment of the duties of her primary function in life. It is not, as the enemies of the woman and enemies of human society claim, that a woman is the equal of a man in work outside the home, and thus have taken her out of the home and separated her from her right duty, and made her perform tasks which are not her true tasks, and then given to others her actual tasks. In this way, they corrupted the family system, and the harmony between the husband and wife has broken down, causing in many cases divorce or remaining together in discontent and unhappiness. Our Shaykh, Muhammad al-Ameen As-Shanqeeti stated in his Tafseer, *Adhwaa al-Bayaan* [3/422]:

> Be aware, may Allaah grant me and you success in doing what He loves and is pleased with, that this erroneous and worthless ideology calling for the

equating of the male and the female in all rulings and areas -- an ideology that is in contradiction to common sense, practical experience, divine revelation and the laws of the Creator (Al-Khaaliq, Al-Baari) - entails in it corruption and disruption of the system of human society which is clear to everyone except to those whom Allaah has blinded their inner sight. This is because Allaah has made the woman, by her specific characteristics, suitable for certain types of participation in the building of human society which a man cannot do, for example pregnancy, childbirth, breastfeeding, the training and upbringing of children and housework, the daily chores, such as cooking, grinding (flour), sweeping and similar things. These services that she provides for the human society in her house, concealed, protected, chaste and observing the qualities of nobleness, virtue and human values, is no less important than the service the man undertakes by providing the means of subsistence. So the (false) claim of the misguided ignorant disbelievers and those who follow them, that the woman must have equal rights in work or in service outside her house to that of a man, even though during the time of her pregnancy and her breastfeeding and her post-birth bleeding she is not able to carry out any action which is difficult, is obvious. If she goes to work like her husband, then the chores of the house are left undone, including the care of young children, breastfeeding of the children who are at that age, and the preparation of food and drink for the man when he returns from work. Then, if another person was hired to carry out these duties, that person would end up being tied up in the house, which is the very thing the woman ran away from, and so the result would be the same. This is in addition to the fact that when a woman leaves her house and works, it leads to the loss of the sense of honour and religion.

So the Muslim sister should fear Allaah and not be taken in by these misleading claims, because indeed the reality of the situation of the women who have been taken in by these allegations is the best witness of the corruption and destruction of these claims - and practical example is the best proof. The Muslim sister should seek to marry while she is still young and desirable, and she should not delay that under the pretext of wishing to continue her education or her career. Instead, a successful marriage is her true happiness and contentment, and it is better than any studies or career. Studies and a career are no substitute for marriage, however high their level.

The Muslim sister should undertake to take care of her house and the upbringing of her children, as this is her basic fruitful function in life and she should not seek a substitute - as nothing can be a substitute. She should not miss the opportunity to marry a righteous man as the Messenger of Allaah, may the peace and blessings of Allaah be upon him said: 'If a man comes to you and you are satisfied with his religiousness and character, then you should marry him. If you do not, there will be great Fitna in the earth and great corruption.' Narrated by Tirmidhi who declared it hasan, while other narrations support it.

Taking the opinion of a woman about her marriage

The woman who is to be married is of three types. She can either be under the age of puberty and a virgin, or above the age of puberty and a virgin, or she may not be a virgin. For each woman, there is a separate ruling:

1. As for the virgin under the age of puberty, there is no disagreement between the scholars that her father can marry her to someone without her consent - as consent in her case is not conceivable. This is because Abu Bakr as-Siddeeq, may Allaah be pleased with him gave his daughter 'A'isha, may Allaah be pleased with her in marriage when she was six years old, and the marriage was consummated when she was nine years old. Agreed upon. Imaam Shawkaani stated in *Nayl al-Awtaar* [6/128-129]:

> This hadeeth is a proof that it is permissible for the father to marry his daughter to somebody before puberty.

He also stated:

> In this there is a proof that it is allowable for a girl under the age of puberty to marry an adult. Imaam Bukhaari devoted a chapter to this and mentioned the hadeeth of 'Aisha, and stated in *al-Fath* the consensus of the scholars on this point.

In *al-Mughni* [6/487]:

> Ibn al-Mundhir says, 'There is a consensus among the People of Knowledge from whom knowledge is taken,

that it is permissible for the father to marry his daughter who has not attained the age of puberty to someone who is suitable.

I say: In the marriage of 'A'isha by Abu Bakr, may Allaah be pleased with both of them when she was six years old to the Prophet, may the peace and blessings of Allaah be upon him is the strongest rebuttal to those who condemn the marriage of a young, pre-pubescent girl to an adult man and revile it, and consider it an evil. This is due entirely to their ignorance or because they intend to cause mischief.

2. As for the virgin who is above the age of puberty, she should not be married off except with her consent - and her consent is her silence, in accordance with the statement of the Prophet, may the peace and blessings of Allaah be upon him: 'The virgin should not be married off until her permission is sought.' They said: 'O Messenger of Allaah, how is her permission sought?' He replied, 'If she remains silent.' Agreed upon. So it is necessary to seek her consent, even if her father is arranging her marriage, according to the most correct conclusion of the two opinions of the scholars. Ibn al-Qayyim stated in *al-Hadi* [5/96]:

> This is the position of the majority of the Salaf and the Madhhab of Abu Haneefah and Ahmad in one of his narrations, and this is the conclusion by which we worship Allaah and do not believe in any other. This position is in accordance with the ruling of the Messenger, may Allaah bless him and grant him peace, his orders, and his prohibitions.

112

3. As for the deflowered woman, she should not be married off unless her consent is sought. Her consent, unlike that of a virgin, must be verbal. In *al-Mughni* [6/493]:

> As for the deflowered woman, we are unaware of any disagreement among the scholars that her consent is verbal. This is proven by narrated accounts, and by the fact that the tongue is the instrument by which what is in the heart is expressed, and it is the thing that is regarded in any situation where approval is stipulated.

Ibn Taymiyyah stated in *Majmu' al-Fataawa* [32/39-40]:

> It is not acceptable for anybody to marry off a woman without her consent, as ordered by the Prophet, may the peace and blessings of Allaah be upon him. If she is forced to marry, she is not obligated to marry unless she is a virgin under the age of puberty, as her father can marry her off and there is no consent for her. As for the adult woman who is not a virgin, it is not permissible for her to be married off without her consent, neither by her father nor anybody else, according to the consensus of the Muslims (the Scholars). In the same way, it is not permitted to give an adult virgin in marriage by other than her father and her grandfather, without her consent by the consensus of the Muslims. As for her father or her grandfather, it is appropriate that they seek her consent. The scholars have differed regarding whether their seeking of her consent is obligatory or mustahabb (preferred) for them; and the correct position is that it is obligatory. It is obligatory upon the guardian of a woman to fear Allaah when he chooses whom to give her in marriage, and he should check the (prospective)

husband to ascertain whether he is suitable or not for the girl, as he is conducting the marriage for her benefit and not for his own benefit.

The condition of a Wali (Gaurdian) in the Woman's Marriage

Giving the woman the right to choose a husband who is suitable does not mean she has complete freedom to marry whomever she wants, even if this was to cause harm for her family and relations. Instead, she is bound by her Wali (Gaurdian) who supervises her decision, advises her, and undertakes the contract of the marriage. She does not conduct the marriage herself. If she does execute the marriage contract herself, the contract is void. This is proven by the hadeeth in *As-Sunan* of 'A'isha, may Allaah be pleased with her: 'Any woman who marries herself off without the permission of her guardian, then her marriage is void, her marriage is void, her marriage is void...' Tirmidhee said this hadeeth is hasan (authentic enough to be accepted). In the four *Sunans*, 'There is no marriage except by a Wali.' These two hadeeths, and others with the same meaning, prove that marriage is not valid without a Wali, because a negating statement negates the validity of that action. Tirmidhee stated (see *al-Mughni* [6/449]):

> The ruling of the people of knowledge, including 'Umar, 'Ali, Ibn 'Abbaas, Abu Hurayrah, may Allah be pleased with all of them, and others is taken from this hadeeth. Likewise, it is narrated from the Scholars of Fiqh of the Taabi'een that they said: 'There is no

marriage unless by a guardian, and this is the position of Shafi'i, Ahmad and Ishaaq...

The ruling concerning beating the Duf (tambourine) by women in order to announce a wedding

It is mustahabb for the women to beat the *duf* (Tambourine) to announce and publicise the wedding. This should take place among women only, and must not be accompanied by music, instruments and female singing. There is no harm for the women to chant poetry on this occasion, as long as men cannot hear them. The Messenger of Allaah, may the peace and blessings of Allaah be upon him said: 'The difference between that which is halaal and that which is haraam is the beating of the tambourine, and the raising of voices during a marriage.' Narrated by the five narrators (Ahmad, Abu Dawud, Nasaa'i', Tirmidhi and Ibn Maajah) except for Abu Dawud, and Tirmidhee declared it hasan. Shawkaani stated in *Nayl al-Awtar* [6/200]:

> This proves that it is permissible during a marriage to beat the Duf and to raise the voices a little with words. For example: 'We have come to you, we have come to you,' et cetera – although not with musical tones that stir up evil desires and contain descriptions of beauty, sin and the consumption of intoxicants. For indeed, these are haraam during a wedding as they are haraam during normal times, and the same ruling applies to all other forms of amusement that are haraam.

The Muslim sister should not waste her money buying jewellery or special clothes for the wedding ceremony, as this is a type of extravagance that Allaah has prohibited, and He informed us that He does not love those who do this. Allaah says:

$$﴿ وَلَا تُسْرِفُوٓا۟ إِنَّهُۥ لَا يُحِبُّ ٱلْمُسْرِفِينَ ﴾$$

"And do not be extravagant, for indeed He does not love the wasteful". [Al-An'am: 141]

So she must be prudent and not extravagant.

The woman's obedience to her husband and the prohibition of her disobedience to him

It is obligatory upon the Muslim woman to obey her husband in that which is halaal. Abu Hurairah, may Allah be pleased with him said: 'The Messenger of Allaah, may the peace and blessings of Allaah be upon him said: "If the woman prays her five salaats, protects her chastity and obeys her husband, she will enter paradise from whichever door she wishes."' Narrated by Ibn Hibbaan in his Saheeh. From Abu Hurairah, may Allah be pleased with him, 'The Messenger of Allaah, may the peace and blessings of Allaah be upon him said: "It is not permissible for the woman to fast while her husband is present, unless she has his permission, and she must not allow anyone into his house unless she has his permission.'" Narrated by Bukhaari and Muslim. From Abu Hurairah, may Allah be pleased with him, 'The Messenger of Allaah, may the peace and blessings of Allaah be upon him said: "If a man asks his wife to go to bed with him, and she does not come to him, and he spends the night angry with her, the angels curse her until the morning."' Narrated by Bukhaari and Muslim and others. In a narration of Bukhaari and Muslim, 'The Messenger of Allaah, may the peace and blessings of Allaah be upon him said: "By He in whose hands my soul is, any man who invites his wife to his bed, and she refuses him, then the One who is above the sky will be angry with her until her husband becomes pleased with her."'

Among the rights of a husband upon his wife is that she looks after his house and does not go outside unless she has his permission. The Prophet, may the peace and blessings of Allaah be upon him said: 'The woman is a gaurdian in the house of her husband, and is responsible for her flock.' Narrated by Bukhaari and Muslim. Among his rights upon her is that she does the housework and does not force him to employ a maid, who could pose a problem (i.e. temptation) for him, and expose him and his children to danger. Ibn Taymiyyah stated in *Majmu' al-Fataawa* [32/260-261]:

Allaah's statement:

﴿ فَٱلصَّٰلِحَٰتُ قَٰنِتَٰتٌ حَٰفِظَٰتٌ لِّلْغَيْبِ بِمَا حَفِظَ ٱللَّهُ ﴾

117

"Therefore the righteous women are devoutly obedient (to Allaah and their husbands), and guard in (the husband's) absence what Allaah orders them to guard (of their chastity and their husbands' property)." [An-Nisa: 34]; indicates the obligation of the woman to obey her husband completely, in terms of serving him, accompanying him on his journeys, and making herself available to him and similar things that have been indicated by the Sunnah of the Messenger of Allaah, may the peace and blessings of Allaah be upon him.

Ibn al-Qayyim stated in *al-Hady* [5-188-189]:

Those who have made it obligatory on the woman to serve her husband have proven this obligation by stating that this is what was commonly practised by those whom Allaah addressed in his statements (i.e. it was the accepted norm of the Prophet, may the peace and blessings of Allaah be upon him and the Sahaaba). As for the provision of ease and luxury to the woman, while the husband serves her and performs the household chores of sweeping, kneading, grinding, mashing (i.e. the preparation of food), and so on, that is all evil. Allaah says:

$$﴿ وَلَهُنَّ مِثْلُ ٱلَّذِى عَلَيْهِنَّ بِٱلْمَعْرُوفِ ﴾$$

"And for women are rights (over their husbands) similar to those (of their husbands) over them, according to what is equitable and just." [Al-Baqara: 228]

And Allaah says:

$$﴿ ٱلرِّجَالُ قَوَّٰمُونَ عَلَى ٱلنِّسَآءِ ﴾$$

"Men are the protectors and maintainers of women" [An-Nisa: 34]

If the woman does not serve him, and instead he becomes her servant, then she becomes the protector and maintainer over him...

... Instead, Allaah made it an obligation on the man to provide her maintenance, clothing, and accomodation in return for the enjoyment he has from her and the service that she provides him - which is dictated by the custom of the people in their culture concerning a married couple.

Also, any open contracts made without stipulated conditions, are subject to the conditions set by local custom, and the custom in this case is that the woman serves her husband, and undertakes the housework.

He also stated:

To make a differentiation between a woman of nobility and a commoner woman, or a rich woman and a poor woman, is not correct, as the best woman of all the worlds (meaning Faatima, may Allah be pleased with herh) used to serve her husband (i.e. no woman, no matter how high her status, or how rich she may be, is better than Faatima, may Allah be pleased with her, the daughter of the Prophet, may the peace and blessings of Allaah be upon him). Once, she came to the Prophet, may the peace and blessings of Allaah be upon him complaining of the difficulty of serving in the house. The Prophet, may the peace and blessings of Allaah be upon him did not relieve her of what she complained of.

If the woman sees that the husband does not want her, but she wishes to remain with him, what can she do to resolve the situation?

Allaah says:

﴿ وَإِنِ امْرَأَةٌ خَافَتْ مِنْ بَعْلِهَا نُشُوزًا أَوْ إِعْرَاضًا فَلَا جُنَاحَ عَلَيْهِمَا أَن يُصْلِحَا بَيْنَهُمَا صُلْحًا وَالصُّلْحُ خَيْرٌ ﴾

"And if a woman fears cruelty or desertion on her husband's part, there is no blame on them if they arrange an amicable settlement between themselves. And such settlement is best." [An-Nisa: 128]

Al-Haafidh Ibn Katheer stated:

If a woman is afraid that her husband will shun her or turn away from her, then it is permissible for her to relinquish all or some of her rights – including her maintennance, clothing, or sexual relations - from the rights that she has upon him. It is permissible for him to accept this from her, so there is no wrong in her relinquishing those rights, and no wrong on him if he accepts this from her. Concerning this, Allaah says:

﴿ فَلَا جُنَاحَ عَلَيْهِمَا أَن يُصْلِحَا بَيْنَهُمَا صُلْحًا وَالصُّلْحُ خَيْرٌ ﴾

"There is no blame on them if they arrange an amicable settlement between themselves. And such settlement is best." [An-Nisa: 128]

Meaning this is better than separation.

Then he related the story of Sawda bint Zam'ah, at the time when she grew old and the Messenger of Allaah, may the peace and blessings of Allaah be upon him wanted to divorce her. She negotiated with him that he retained her while she gave her night (of sleeping with him) to 'Aisha and he accepted and retained her upon this agreement.

See *Tafseer Ibn Katheer* [2/406, last edition].

If the woman hates the man and she does not wish to remain with him, what could she do?

Allaah says:

﴿ فَإِنْ خِفْتُمْ أَلَّا يُقِيمَا حُدُودَ ٱللَّهِ فَلَا جُنَاحَ عَلَيْهِمَا فِيمَا ٱفْتَدَتْ بِهِۦ ﴾

"If you do indeed fear that they would be unable to keep the limits ordained by Allaah, there is no blame on either of them if she gives something (all or part of her bridal money) for her freedom (divorce)." [Al-Baqara: 229]

Al-Hafidh Ibn Katheer stated in his Tafseer [1/483]:

If the husband and wife are in discord with one another, and the woman does not provide the rights of the man and she hates him, is unable to live with him, then she is allowed to release herself from him by returning what he gave her (her bridal money). There is no problem in her returning this to him, and no problem if he accepts it from her. This is known as *al-khul'u*.

If the woman asks her husband for a divorce without any valid reason, what punishment does she deserve?

Narrated from Thawbaan, may Allaah be pleased with him: 'The Prophet, may the peace and blessings of Allaah be upon him said: "Any woman who asks her husband for a divorce without a valid reason, then the fragrance of the Jannah (Paradise is prohibited for her" Narrated by Abu Dawud and Tirmidhee, and Ibn Hibbaan declared it hasan in his Saheeh. This is because the most hateful halaal action to Allaah is divorce. Divorce is only to be used as a last resort, and if it is used before that, it is disliked because of the harm it causes – which is a well-known fact. The need or situation which drives a woman to seek a divorce is that her husband is not fulfilling her rights to such a degree that it becomes a detriment for her to remain with him. Allaah says:

$$﴿ فَإِمْسَاكٌ بِمَعْرُوفٍ أَوْ تَسْرِيحٌ بِإِحْسَانٍ ﴾$$

"Either you retain her on equitable terms, or separate from her with kindness." [Al-Baqara: 229]

Allaah also says:

$$﴿ لِلَّذِينَ يُؤْلُونَ مِن نِّسَآئِهِمْ تَرَبُّصُ أَرْبَعَةِ أَشْهُرٍ فَإِن فَآءُو فَإِنَّ ٱللَّهَ$$

$$غَفُورٌ رَّحِيمٌ ۝ وَإِنْ عَزَمُواْ ٱلطَّلَـٰقَ فَإِنَّ ٱللَّهَ سَمِيعٌ عَلِيمٌ ﴾$$

"For those who take an oath of abstention from (sexual relations with) their wives, a waiting for four months is ordained; if then they return, Allaah is Oft-forgiving, Most Merciful. But if their intention is firm for divorce, then Allaah hears and knows all things." [Al-Baqara: 226, 227]

What the woman must do after the termination of her marriage

There are two types of separation between husband and wife. The first occurs during life, the second by death. For both types of separation, the woman must wait for a fixed period of time set by the Shari'ah, during which she may not remarry. This is known as the 'Iddah. The wisdom behind the 'Iddah is that she is still bound by the marriage to ensure that she is not pregnant, so that someone other than the husband from whom she became separated does not have sexual intercourse with her. If

123

she were to become pregnant, there would be confusion over who the father was, and the right of descendency would be lost. Also, the 'Iddah is a token of respect for the previous marriage and for the honour of the ex-husband or late husband, and demonstrates the effect of the separation on the woman.

There are four types of 'Iddah. The first type is the 'Iddah of a pregnant woman which always ends with childbirth, whether the divorce was final[6], or the divorce was reversible[7], the separation being from a living husband, or a dead one. Allaah says:

$$﴿ وَأُوْلَٰتُ ٱلْأَحْمَالِ أَجَلُهُنَّ أَن يَضَعْنَ حَمْلَهُنَّ ﴾$$

"And for those who are pregnant, their prescribed period is until they deliver their babies." [Al-Talaq: 4]

The second type is the 'Iddah of the divorced woman who menstruates (i.e. before menopause). Its duration is three menstrual periods. Allaah says:

$$﴿ وَٱلْمُطَلَّقَٰتُ يَتَرَبَّصْنَ بِأَنفُسِهِنَّ ثَلَٰثَةَ قُرُوٓءٍ ﴾$$

---

6 The occurence of the 'final' type of divorce means that the man cannot remarry the woman except with a new marriage contract and she has given her consent. There are several instances for that, and they are clearly stated in the books of *fiqh*.

7 The 'reversible' type of divorce allows the man to take back the woman in marriage even without her consent, and without making a new marriage contract.

"Divorced women shall make themselves wait (from getting married to a new husband) for three monthly periods." [Al-Baqara: 228]

The third type is the 'Iddah of the woman who does not menstruate and she can be of two types; a young girl under the age of puberty, meaning that she has not started to menstruate, or an elderly woman who has stopped menstruating. Allaah has decreed the 'Iddah of both types of women in His statement:

$$﴿ وَٱلَّـٰٓئِى يَئِسْنَ مِنَ ٱلْمَحِيضِ مِن نِّسَآئِكُمْ إِنِ ٱرْتَبْتُمْ فَعِدَّتُهُنَّ ثَلَـٰثَةُ أَشْهُرٍ وَٱلَّـٰٓئِى لَمْ يَحِضْنَ ﴾$$

"Such of your women as have passed the age of monthly courses, for them the prescribed period, if you have any doubts, is three months, and for those who have not started menstruating (it is likewise the same)." [Al-Talaq: 4]

The fourth type is the woman whose husband has died. Allaah has decreed her 'Iddah by His statement:

$$﴿ وَٱلَّذِينَ يُتَوَفَّوْنَ مِنكُمْ وَيَذَرُونَ أَزْوَٰجًا يَتَرَبَّصْنَ بِأَنفُسِهِنَّ أَرْبَعَةَ أَشْهُرٍ وَعَشْرًا ﴾$$

"And those of you who die and leave behind widows, they (the widows) shall make themselves wait (from getting married after the death of their husbands) for four months and ten days." [Al-Baqara: 234]

This includes the woman who had had sexual intercourse with her husband and the woman who had not, the pre-pubescent woman, and the older woman who has stopped menstruating, but does not include the pregnant woman, because she has been excluded by Allaah's statement:

$$ ﴿ وَأُوْلَٰتُ ٱلْأَحْمَالِ أَجَلُهُنَّ أَن يَضَعْنَ حَمْلَهُنَّ ﴾ $$

"And for those who are pregnant, their prescribed period is until they deliver their babies." [Al-Talaq: 4]

Taken from *al-Hady an-Nabawi* [594/595] by Ibn Qayyim, authenticated edition.

The Prohibitions Applicable to the Woman in Her 'Iddah

1. The Ruling Concerning Marriage Proposals To Her

i) In a reversible divorce, it is haraam to propose to the woman, explicitly or by indication. This is because she is treated as if she is still married; therefore it is not permissible for anyone to propose to her as she is still in the custody of her husband.

ii) In a final divorce, it is haraam to propose to the woman explicitly, but it is allowed to make an indication as Allaah said:

﴿ وَلَا جُنَاحَ عَلَيْكُمْ فِيمَا عَرَّضْتُم بِهِۦ مِنْ خِطْبَةِ ٱلنِّسَآءِ أَوْ أَكْنَنتُمْ فِىٓ أَنفُسِكُمْ ﴾

"And there is no blame on you if you make a hint of betrothal or conceal it in your hearts." [Al-Baqara: 235]

A clear or explicit proposal is the one made by clearly expressing the wish to marry the woman, for example by saying, 'I want to marry you.' This is because her concern to get re-married again may lead her to inform him that her 'Iddah is over before it is actually over. This is unlike a proposal that is hinted or indicated, because it is not emphatic in displaying the wish to marry her, and therefore does not create this situation. Furthermore the understanding of the above verse shows this.

An example of a hint or indication is like saying: 'I am interested in someone like you.' It is allowable for the woman in her 'Iddah after a final divorce to answer the hinted proposal with an indication or a hint. But it is not allowable for her to reply to a clear and explicit proposal. Finally, it is not allowable for a woman who is in her 'Iddah after a reversible divorce to answer any proposal, whether it is explicit or hinted.

127

2. It is haraam for a woman to contract a marriage with someone during her' Iddah.

This is because of the saying of Allah, The Most High:

﴿ وَلَا تَعْزِمُوا عُقْدَةَ ٱلنِّكَاحِ حَتَّىٰ يَبْلُغَ ٱلْكِتَٰبُ أَجَلَهُ ﴾

"And do not resolve on the tie of marriage till the term prescribed is fulfilled." [Al-Baqara: 235]

Ibn Katheer stated in his Tafseer [1/509]:

This means: 'do not make any contracts for marriage until the 'Iddah has finished'. There is a consensus among the scholars that the contract is not valid if it takes place during the time of the 'Iddah.

Note: Two important facts

1. The woman who is divorced before the consummation of her marriage with her husband does not have an 'Iddah by the statement of Allaah:

﴿ يَٰٓأَيُّهَا ٱلَّذِينَ ءَامَنُوٓا إِذَا نَكَحْتُمُ ٱلْمُؤْمِنَٰتِ ثُمَّ طَلَّقْتُمُوهُنَّ مِن قَبْلِ أَن تَمَسُّوهُنَّ فَمَا لَكُمْ عَلَيْهِنَّ مِنْ عِدَّةٍ تَعْتَدُّونَهَا ﴾

"O you who believe! When you marry believing women and then divorce them before having sexual

128

intercourse with them, no period of 'Iddah have you to count in respect of them." [Al-Ahzab: 49]

Ibn Katheer stated in his Tafseer [5/479]:

There is a consensus on this point among the scholars; if a woman is divorced before having intercourse with her husband, she does not have an 'Iddah and can go and marry as soon as she wishes.

2. If the woman is divorced before having intercourse with the husband, and yet the bridal money has already been fixed, then she takes half of it. Any woman, who is divorced without her bridal money being fixed, is entitled to a compensation of an appropriate amount of clothes or similar things. The woman that is divorced after intercourse with the husband receives the bridal money in full.

Allaah says:

﴿ لَّا جُنَاحَ عَلَيْكُمْ إِن طَلَّقْتُمُ ٱلنِّسَآءَ مَا لَمْ تَمَسُّوهُنَّ أَوْ تَفْرِضُوا لَهُنَّ فَرِيضَةً وَمَتِّعُوهُنَّ عَلَى ٱلْمُوسِعِ قَدَرُهُ وَعَلَى ٱلْمُقْتِرِ قَدَرُهُ ﴾

"There is no blame on you if you divorce women before consummation of marriage, or the fixation of their bridal money; but bestow on them (a suitable gift), the wealthy according to his means, and the poor according to his means - " [Al-Baqara: 236]

To His saying:

$$\textarabic{﴿ وَإِن طَلَّقْتُمُوهُنَّ مِن قَبْلِ أَن تَمَسُّوهُنَّ وَقَدْ فَرَضْتُمْ لَهُنَّ}$$

$$\textarabic{فَرِيضَةً فَنِصْفُ مَا فَرَضْتُمْ ﴾}$$

"And if you divorce them before consummation, but after the fixation of a bridal money for them, then the half of the bridal money (is due to them)." [Al-Baqara: 237]

Meaning that there is no harm upon you husbands, to divorce women before having intercourse with them, and before fixing the bridal money, and if there is in that a dissapointment for her, then it is made up by his being obliged to pay the mut'ah (compensation), the amount of which is specified on every husband according to his position of wealth or poverty. Then Allaah mentioned the woman whose bridal money was fixed and ordered that half of it be given to her. Al-Haafidh Ibn Katheer stated in his Tafseer [1/512]:

> And the halving of the bridal money in this situation is an issue upon which there is a consensus among the scholars without any dissagreement between them.

3. The impermissible things for a woman in 'Iddah after the death of her husband

Five things are not permissible for the woman who is in 'Iddah after the death of her husband. This is known as Ihdaad (mourning).

i) All types of perfume. She should not apply perfume to her body or clothes or use anything that is perfumed. This is by the statement of the Prophet, may the peace and blessings of Allaah be upon him in an authentic hadeeth: 'She should not touch perfume.'

ii) Beautification of her body. It is prohibited for her to dye her hands and feet with henna and all types of beautification, such as *kohl* (eyeliner) and different types of skin dye, unless she is forced to use kohl for medicinal purposes and not beautification, in which case she is allowed to use it at night and remove it during the day. There is no harm if she uses medicine for her eyes that contains no beautification.

iii) Beautification with clothes designed to beautify. She should wear plain clothes that do not contain beautification although there is no set colour for her to wear as is set by local custom, for example black.

iv) Wearing jewellery of any type, even rings.

v) Sleeping anywhere other than the home in which her husband died and left her residing in it. And she cannot move anywhere else unless she has a reason that is valid Islaamically, and she should not leave to visit the sick, or to visit a friend, or a relative. It is permissible for her to leave during the day for absolutely essential requirements.

Nothing else, apart from these five things, is prohibited from the things that Allaah has made permissible for her. Imaam Ibn al-Qayyim stated in *al-Hady an-Nabawi* [5/507]:

> She is not prohibited from cutting her nails and plucking the hair of her armpits and cutting the hair which is preferred to be cut nor from bathing with lotus leaves and combing her hair with it.

Ibn Taymiyyah stated in *Majmu' al-Fataawa* [34/27-28]:

> It is permissible for her to eat anything that Allaah has made permissible, like fruit and meat, and also any drink that is permissible...

> ... And she is not prohibited from doing any kind of work that is permissible, for example embroidery, sewing, spinning and other things which women do. All things which are normally permissible for her outside the 'Iddah period are allowable for her, for example speaking to those she has a need to speak to among men, if she is covered, and other things. This point that I have mentioned is the Sunnah of the Messenger of Allaah, may the peace and blessings of Allaah be upon him which the women of the Sahaaba used to do when their husbands died.

What the lay people say: that she should cover her face from the moon and not climb the roof of her house, and not talk to men, and that she should shield her face in front of her mahrams, and similar things, none of these have any proof, and Allaah knows best.

Chapter 10

Laws Which Protect The Nobility & Chastity Of A Woman

The woman, like the man, is ordered to lower her gaze and remain chaste. Allaah says:

﴿ قُل لِّلْمُؤْمِنِينَ يَغُضُّوا مِنْ أَبْصَـٰرِهِمْ وَيَحْفَظُوا فُرُوجَهُمْ ذَٰلِكَ أَزْكَىٰ لَهُمْ إِنَّ ٱللَّهَ خَبِيرٌ بِمَا يَصْنَعُونَ ۝ وَقُل لِّلْمُؤْمِنَـٰتِ يَغْضُضْنَ مِنْ أَبْصَـٰرِهِنَّ وَيَحْفَظْنَ فُرُوجَهُنَّ ﴾

"Tell the believing men to lower their gaze (from looking at forbidden things) and guard their private parts (from forbidden sexual acts). That is purer for them. Verily Allaah is well acquainted with all that they do. And tell the believing women to lower their gaze (from looking at forbidden things) and guard their private parts (from forbidden sexual acts)." [An-Nur: 30, 31]

Our respected Shaykh, Muhammad Ameen ash-Shanqeetee, may Allaah have mercy on him stated in his Tafseer, *Adhwaa al-Bayaan*:

Allaah the Almighty and Most High has ordered the believing men and women to lower their gaze, and remain chaste, which includes abstaining from fornication, sodomy (homosexuality), lesbianism, nakedness and exposing the private parts in front of people...

... Allaah has promised those who obey His order in this verse, among both men and women, with forgiveness and a great reward, if they also adopt the qualities mentioned in Sura al-Ahzaab, in the statement of Allah:

﴿ إِنَّ ٱلْمُسْلِمِينَ وَٱلْمُسْلِمَٰتِ ﴾

"Verily the Muslim (those who submit to Allah in Islam) men and women," to His saying:

﴿ وَٱلْحَٰفِظِينَ فُرُوجَهُمْ وَٱلْحَٰفِظَٰتِ وَٱلذَّٰكِرِينَ ٱللَّهَ كَثِيرًا وَٱلذَّٰكِرَٰتِ أَعَدَّ ٱللَّهُ لَهُم مَّغْفِرَةً وَأَجْرًا عَظِيمًا ﴾

"And the men and the women who guard their chastity, and the men and the women who remember Allaah much (with their hearts and tongues), for them Allaah has prepared forgiveness and a great reward." [Al-Ahzab: 35]

He also stated in *Adhwaa al Bayaan*:

... And lesbianism is the sexual relation that takes place between two women by the rubbing of their bodies. This is a terrible sin, with both the women involved deserving a harsh punishment (as a deterrent).

In *al-Mughni* [8/198]:

134

... And if two women rub one another sexually, then they are both cursed fornicators, as is proved by the statement of the Prophet, may the peace and blessings of Allaah be upon him that he said: 'If a woman sexually approaches another woman they are both fornicators', and they both deserve a punishment set by the ruler, as this is a type of fornication for which there is no prescribed punishment. [8]

So Muslim women, particularly the younger women, should be warned against committing this vile sin.

As for lowering the gaze, Ibn al-Qayyim said regarding this duty in his book *al-Jawaab al-Kaafee* [pp. 129-130]:

... Regarding the stray glances, they are the scouts and messengers of lust, and guarding against them is the basis of protection of chastity. Whoever looks (at a member of the opposite sex), exposes himself to the sources of ruin. The Prophet, may the peace and blessings of Allaah be upon him said: "O 'Ali, the stray glance should not be followed with another glance, as the first one (only) is permissible for you.' The meaning of a 'stray glance' is the glance which takes place involuntarily, and not on purpose. In *al-Musnad*, narrated from the Prophet, may the peace and blessings of Allaah be upon him: 'The glance is one of the poisoned arrows of Iblees (Shaytaan)'...

---

8 Ibn Taymiyyah stated in *Majmu' al-Fataawa* (15/321): 'And in the light of this, the lesbian woman is a fornicator, as in the hadeeth, "The fornication of women is lesbianism."'

... And the glance is the cause of most of the troubles which befall a human being, as a stray glance creates a dangerous impulse, the impulse becomes an evil thought; the thought leads to desire; the desire brings about an evil intention, which becomes stronger until it becomes a powerful urge, thus an action takes place, inevitably, if there is nothing to prevent it. For this reason it is said: 'to have patience in lowering ones gaze is easier than bearing the pain which may come after...'

So it is upon the Muslim woman to lower and avert her gaze from men, and not look at the provocative pictures which are found in various media, magazines, TV and video, in order to protect herself from evil consequences; for how many times have unguarded glances caused the lover grief and sorrow, and how many a fire have started from a small spark?

2. Another means by which a woman's chastity can be protected is by avoiding listening to songs, and flutes (i.e. music). Imaam Ibn Qayyim stated in *Igaathat al-Lahfaan* [1/242, 238, 264, 265]:

Among the tricks of the Shaytaan by which he deceives those who have little knowledge, wisdom or religiousness, and by which he entraps the hearts of the ignorant and the wrongdoers is listening to whistling, clapping, and music with prohibited instruments which divert the hearts from the Qur'aan, and makes them devoted to sin and disobedience, and thus is the 'quraan' of the Shaytaan; a thick barrier from Al-Rahmaan, and the charm of homosexuality and fornication. By it, the sinful lover gains from his beloved one the aim of his desire...

... As for listening to the woman or effeminate men, this is one of the worst sins and one of the most potent ways in which religion is corrupted...

... And there is no doubt that the conscientious man will prevent his family from listening to music, in the same way he keeps them away from sources of ill repute...

He also stated:

It is well known among people that if a man finds it difficult to gain the favor of a woman, he tries hard to make her listen to music in order that she may soften towards him. This is because women are very sensitive to sound. If the sound is music, she is aroused in two ways: from the sound itself and from its meaning.

He also stated:

If these charms were combined with drums, flutes, and effeminite erotic dancing, then the woman, if she were to be ensnared by any music, would be ensnared by *this* music. By Allaah the Eternal! How many a free woman has been turned into a whore through music...

So the Muslim woman should fear Allaah and be warned of this dangerous sickness of character; listening to music which is distributed among the Muslims by many means and in various forms, which has caused many ignorant girls to try and obtain it from its distributors and exchange it with one another.

3. Among the means of preserving chastity is to prevent the woman from travelling unless she has a mahram to protect her from the desires of the licentious and the sinful. Authentic hadeeths prohibit the travel of a

woman without a mahram. Among them is the hadeeth narrated by Ibn 'Umar, may Allaah be pleased with him. He said: 'The Messenger of Allaah, may the peace and blessings of Allaah be upon him said: 'A woman must not travel for more than three days unless she is accompanied by a mahram.' Agreed upon. Abu Sa'eed, may Allaah be pleased with him narrated that, 'The Prophet, may the peace and blessings of Allaah be upon him prohibited a woman to travel the distance of two days or two nights unless her husband or a mahram accompanied her.' Agreed upon. From Abu Hurairah, may Allah be pleased with him, 'The Prophet, may the peace and blessings of Allaah be upon him said: "It is not permissible for a woman to travel the distance of a day and a night unless she is accompanied by a mahram.'" Agreed upon.

The intended meaning in these hadeeths of 'three days,' 'two days,' and 'a day and a night,' is by the means of transport that were in use at that time, including travel by foot and on mounted animals. The apparent difference between these hadeeths of the distance being three days, or two days, or a night and a day, or less, has been answered by the scholars as meaning that the woman is prohibited from anything that is considered as 'travel'.

Imaam Nawawi stated in *Sharh Saheeh Muslim* [9/103]:

> ... So the conclusion is that for anything considered as a journey, the woman is prohibited from it, unless she is not accompanied by her husband or a mahram, whether

it is for three days, two days, a day and a night, or other than that, because of the narration of Ibn Abbaas, (the meaning of) which is general, and is the last of the narrations of Imaam Muslim which have preceded: 'The woman must not travel unless she is accompanied by a mahram.' This includes anything regarded as travel, and Allaah knows best.

As for those who have issued fatwaas permitting the woman to travel with a group of women for an obligatory Hajj, this is not in accordance with the Sunnah, as Imaam al-Khattaabi stated in *Ma'aalim as-Sunan* [2/276-277] with the *Tahtheeb* (condensation) of Ibn al-Qayyim:

The Prophet, may the peace and blessings of Allaah be upon him warned the woman from travelling unless she had a man as her mahram. Thus, the permissibility of her leaving to travel for Hajj without the condition set by the Prophet, may the peace and blessings of Allaah be upon him is not in accordance with the Sunnah. So, if her leaving without a mahram is a sin, it is not permissible for her to begin her Hajj, as it consitutes obeying an order (from Allaah) that will lead to disobeying Him.

I say, while they themselves have not permitted the woman to travel without a mahram under all circumstances, instead they only permitted her to travel for an obligatory Hajj alone, as Imaam Nawawi stated in *al-Majmu'* [8/249]:

It is (i.e. the woman's travel) not permissible for non-obligatory worship, commercial expeditions, or visiting, etc. unless accompanied by a mahram.

As for those who have become careless in this time regarding a woman travelling without a mahram for any types of travel, not a single scholar whose opinion is acceptable agrees with them. They claim that her mahram will place her in the plane then another mahram will meet her when she arrives and she reaches the country she intends, because the plane, they claim, is a safe place as there are many passengers, both men and women.

Our reply to them is: Certainly not, as the plane is even more dangerous than other forms of transport, because the passengers mix freely and she might sit next to a man. Perhaps the plane will be diverted to another airport and she will not find anyone to receive her and will thus be exposed to danger. What would be the fate of a woman stranded in a country she doesn't know, without a mahram?

4. Another means of protecting chastity is the prohibition of the seclusion of a woman with a man who is not her mahram. The Prophet, may the peace and blessings of Allaah be upon him said: "Whoever believes in Allaah and the Last Day, should not allow himself to be alone with a woman who is not accompanied by a mahram, because the third person present will be the Shaytaan." It is narrated from 'Aamir Ibn Rabee'ah, may Allaah be pleased with him that he said: 'The Messenger of Allaah, may the peace and blessings of Allaah be upon him said: "It is not permissible for a man to be alone with a woman who is not permissible for him, for indeed the third person with

them will be the Shaytaan, unless the third of them is a mahram.'" Al-Majd stated in al-Muntaqaa.' (These two hadeeth were) narrated by Ahmad and is preceded by a hadeeth with the same meaning from Ibn 'Abbaas, may Allaah be pleased with him which is agreed upon.

Imaam Shawkaani stated in *Nayl al-Awtaar* [6/120]:

There is a consensus on the prohibition of seclusion with a woman as has been quoted by al-Haafidh in *al-Fath*. The reason for the prohibition is what is mentioned in the hadeeth that the third of them is the Shaytaan, and it is his presence that causes them to sin. And as for having a mahram present, then being with the woman is permissible because the occurrence of sin is stopped by his presence.

Some women and their guardians are careless with certain types of seclusion:

i) The seclusion of a woman with the relative of her husband, and her revealing her face in front of him. This type of seclusion is more dangerous than others. The Prophet, may the peace and blessings of Allaah be upon him said: 'Beware of entering the presence of women.' So a man from the Ansaar said: 'O Messenger of Allaah, and what about her brother-in-law ('al-hamwu') ?' He (the Prophet, may the peace and blessings of Allaah be upon him) said: 'The brother-in-law is death.' Narrated by Ahmad, Bukhaari, At-Tirmidhee who authenticated it. He said: 'the meaning of the word 'al hamwu': it is said he is the brother of the husband. It is as if he disliked her to be alone with him.' al-Haafidh Ibn Hajar stated in *Fath al-Baari* [9/331]:

An-Nawawi said: 'The scholars of Arabic Language have agreed that the ahmaa (plural of hamwu) are the relatives of the husband of the woman such as his father, uncle, brother, nephew, cousin and others like them. And its meaning in the context of the hadeeth is the husband's male relatives excluding his father and their fathers and his son and their sons, as they are all mahrams for his wife, and it is permissible for them to be alone with her; these are not described as being death.'

He said:

The customs of the people have become lax; a man may seclude himself with the wife of his brother and as he might assume his place after his brother's death (i.e. he could marry her), he is therefore more deserving to be prohibited.

Shawkaani stated in *Nayl al-Awtar* [6/122]:

His statement, 'al-hamwu is death,' means that the danger from him is greater than from others in the same way that the fear of death is greater than fear of anything else.

So the Muslim sister should fear Allaah and not become careless in this area, even if the people themselves have become careless. This is because the deciding factor for any situation is the ruling of the Shari'ah and not the custom of the people.

ii) Some women and their guardians have become careless or lax by allowing the woman to be alone in a car with the driver who is not her mahram, even though this is the type of seclusion which is prohibited. Shaykh Muhammad ibn Ibraheem Aal As-Shaykh, the Mufti of Saudi Arabia, stated in *Majmu' al-Fataawa* [10/52]:

> Now no doubt remains that the entry of a woman into a car alone with the driver of the car, without a mahram to accompany her, is a blatant evil. It contains many evils that should not be underestimated, even if the woman is a modest young woman or a chaste woman who speaks to men. The man who allows this to happen to the women of his family is weak in his religion, deficient in his manliness, and has little honor with respect to his family. The Prophet, may the peace and blessings of Allaah be upon him said: 'Never is a man left alone with a woman except that the Shaytaan is the third of them.'

Her travel in a car with a man is worse then being alone with him in a house, or situations like it. This is because he is able to go with her wherever he wishes, inside or outside the country, with or without her approval. This creates many evils much worse than simply being secluded with a woman in a house.

It is imperative that the male who is her mahram who accompanies her to prevent this seclusion is an adult. It is not sufficient for a child to be with her. Some women think that if a child accompanies them, then seclusion is prevented, although this is an incorrect view. Imaam Nawawi stated [9/109]:

> If a man and a woman seclude themselves without a third person being present, this is haraam by the agreement of the scholars. The same ruling applies if those who are not feared, because of their young age

143

accompanied her; the state of the seclusion being haraam still remains.

iii) Some women and their guardians have become lax regarding the woman visiting a doctor for treatment. This is a great evil and a great danger, and it is not permissible to allow it to happen and remain silent. Shaykh Muhammad ibn Ibraaheem stated in *Majmu' al-Fataawa* [10/13]:

> In any case, seclusion with a woman is haraam Islaamically, even if the man were a doctor who is treating her, from the hadeeth 'Never is a man left alone with a woman except that the Shaytaan is the third of them.' So it is imperative that someone be with her, either her husband or one of her male guardians. If none are available, then at least one of her women relations, and if there is no one to accompany her from among those mentioned, and her sickness is dangerous or severe, and it is not possible to delay it, then at the very least, she should be accompanied by a female nurse or someone like her in order to avoid seclusion, which is prohibited.

Also, it is not permissible for a woman to be alone with a doctor, even if she herself is a female doctor who is a colleague, or a nurse; or a blind teacher with a female student; or an air hostess with a man who is not one of her mahrams. These are areas in which people have become lax in the name of so-called (actually false) 'civilization' and blind following of the disbelievers and out of negligence with the laws of the Shari'ah! There is no power and no strength except with Allaah, the High, the Mighty.

It is not allowable for a man to be alone with a maid who is employed in his house, or for a man's wife to be alone with a male domestic helper. The problem concerning domestic helpers is a severe one that has afflicted many people today, due to the preoccupation of women with studies and work outside the home. This makes it necessary for the believers, both men and women to be extremely careful, and to take all necessary precautions and not to adopt corrupt customs.

Finally, it is prohibited for a woman to shake hands with a man who is not her mahram. Shaykh Abdul Azeez Ibn Abdullah Ibn Baaz, the General President of Iftaa, Da'wah and Guidance, said in *Majmu' al-Fataawa* printed by the Establishment of ad-Da'wah al-Islaamiyyah as-Sahafiyyah [1/185]:

> It is not permissible for women to shake hands with other than their mahrams at all, whether they are young or old and whether the person she greets is a youth or an old man, as this entails the danger of Fitna affecting every person involved. It has been authentically reported about the Messenger of Allaah, may the peace and blessings of Allaah be upon him: 'The hand of the Messenger of Allaah, may the peace and blessings of Allaah be upon him never touched the hand of a woman ever. He used to take their pledge of allegiance by word of mouth alone.' There is no difference between whether she shakes his hand with or without a cover because of the generality of the proofs, and to prevent the means by which fitna can take place.

Shaykh Muhammad al-Ameen Ash-Shanqeetee, in his Tafseer *Adhwaa al-Bayaan*, stated [6/602-603]:

Know that it is not permissible for a man to shake the hand of a woman and it is not permissible for any part of his body to touch any part of her body. The proof of this is that:

Firstly, it has been established that the Prophet, may the peace and blessings of Allaah be upon him said: 'Indeed, I do not shake the hands of women...' and Allaah says:

$$\textARABIC{﴿ لَّقَدۡ كَانَ لَكُمۡ فِى رَسُولِ ٱللَّهِ أُسۡوَةٌ حَسَنَةٌ ﴾}$$

'You have indeed in the Messenger of Allaah a perfect example'.

So we are enjoined not to shake the hands of women in obedience and adherence to the Sunnah of the Prophet, may the peace and blessings of Allaah be upon him. The hadeeth that we have mentioned has previously been mentioned in Surah al-Hajj regarding the prohibition of wearing brightly coloured clothes at all times, in Ihraam and outside of Ihraam for men, and in Surah al-Ahzaab regarding the verse of the Hijaab. The fact that the Prophet, may the peace and blessings of Allaah be upon him did not shake the hands of women even at the time of receiving the oath of allegiance is a clear proof that a man should not shake the hand of a woman, nor should any part of his body touch any part of hers, because the merest form of physical contact is to shake hands. So if the Prophet, may the peace and blessings of Allaah be upon him abstained from this physical contact at a time in which it was most appropriate, that is the time of receiving the pledge of allegiance, this indicates that it is prohibited. It is not for anyone to go against the Prophet, may the peace and blessings of Allaah be upon him as he is the one who sets laws for this nation (Ummah) by his actions, statements, and silent approval.

The second point is what we have previously mentioned - that a woman is 'awrah (a body which is to be covered) completely, and that it is obligatory for her to wear Hijaab, and that the order to lower the gaze is due to the danger of fitna occuring. There is no doubt that a physical contact between two bodies creates a stronger instinct, and a stronger lure towards Fitna than a look by the eyes. Any sensible person knows that.

The third point is that this is a means by which gratification is gained from a woman, due to the lack of taqwa (fear of Allah) in these times, the lack of religious duty, and slackness in avoidance of dubious acts. We have been informed many times that some men kiss their wives' sisters, mouth to mouth, and they call this type of kissing, which is haraam by the consensus of the 'Ulema a 'form of greeting'! You hear them say: 'Greet her,' meaning: 'Kiss her'. The truth however, of which there is no doubt, is to distance oneself from all forms of Fitna and doubtful things and their causes. Among the greatest causes of Fitna is for a man to touch any part of a woman. Thus any pretext which leads to actions which are haraam must be stopped."

To conclude, the believing men and women should remember the guidance of Allaah to them in His statement:

﴿ قُل لِّلْمُؤْمِنِينَ يَغُضُّوا۟ مِنْ أَبْصَٰرِهِمْ وَيَحْفَظُوا۟ فُرُوجَهُمْ ذَٰلِكَ أَزْكَىٰ لَهُمْ إِنَّ ٱللَّهَ خَبِيرٌۢ بِمَا يَصْنَعُونَ ۝ وَقُل لِّلْمُؤْمِنَٰتِ يَغْضُضْنَ مِنْ أَبْصَٰرِهِنَّ وَيَحْفَظْنَ فُرُوجَهُنَّ وَلَا يُبْدِينَ زِينَتَهُنَّ إِلَّا مَا ظَهَرَ مِنْهَا وَلْيَضْرِبْنَ بِخُمُرِهِنَّ عَلَىٰ جُيُوبِهِنَّ وَلَا يُبْدِينَ زِينَتَهُنَّ إِلَّا لِبُعُولَتِهِنَّ أَوْ ءَابَآئِهِنَّ أَوْ ءَابَآءِ بُعُولَتِهِنَّ أَوْ أَبْنَآئِهِنَّ أَوْ أَبْنَآءِ بُعُولَتِهِنَّ أَوْ إِخْوَٰنِهِنَّ أَوْ بَنِىٓ إِخْوَٰنِهِنَّ أَوْ بَنِىٓ أَخَوَٰتِهِنَّ أَوْ نِسَآئِهِنَّ أَوْ مَا مَلَكَتْ أَيْمَٰنُهُنَّ أَوِ ٱلتَّٰبِعِينَ غَيْرِ أُو۟لِى ٱلْإِرْبَةِ مِنَ ٱلرِّجَالِ أَوِ ٱلطِّفْلِ ٱلَّذِينَ لَمْ يَظْهَرُوا۟ عَلَىٰ عَوْرَٰتِ ٱلنِّسَآءِ وَلَا يَضْرِبْنَ بِأَرْجُلِهِنَّ لِيُعْلَمَ مَا يُخْفِينَ مِن زِينَتِهِنَّ وَتُوبُوٓا۟ إِلَى ٱللَّهِ جَمِيعًا أَيُّهَ ٱلْمُؤْمِنُونَ لَعَلَّكُمْ تُفْلِحُونَ ۝ ﴾

"Tell the believing men to lower their gaze (from looking at forbidden things) and guard their chastity. That is purer for them. Verily Allaah is well acquainted with all that they do. And tell the believing women to lower their gaze (from looking at forbidden things) and guard their chastity, and not display their adornment except what (must ordinarily) appear thereof; and they should draw their veils over their bosoms, and not display their adornment except to their husbands, or their fathers, or their husbands' fathers, or their sons, or their husbands' sons, or their brothers, or their brothers' sons, or their sisters' sons, or their (Muslim) women, or the slaves whom their right hands possess, or simple-minded male servants free of sexual desires, or small children who have no sense of feminine sex. And they should not strike their feet in order to draw attention to their hidden ornaments. And all of you ask Allaah to forgive you all, O believers, that you may attain bliss." [An-Nur: 30, 31]

And all praises be to the Lord of the Worlds, and may Allaah bless our Prophet Muhammad, his family and companions and grant them peace.

تم طبعه في وزارة الشؤون الإسلامية والأوقاف والدعوة والإرشاد

على نفقة مؤسسة إبراهيم بن عبد العزيز البراهيم الخيرية

تنبيهات
على
أحكام تختص بالمؤمنات

تأليف فضيلة الشيخ

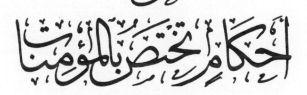

د. صالح بن فوزان بن عبد الله الفوزان

عضو هيئة كبار العلماء

وعضو اللجنة الدائمة للإفتاء والبحوث العلمية

باللغة الإنجليزية

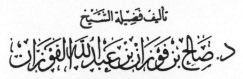

أشرفت وكالة الوزارة لشؤون المطبوعات والنشر بالوزارة على إصداره

١٤٢٢هـ